Dear Carol,
    Hope you have many happy
hours reading this.
        All our love,
            Colin, Barbara, Bill, Coral
        & Andrew

THE DIARY OF IRIS VAUGHAN

THE DIARY

of

IRIS VAUGHAN

HOWARD TIMMINS

CAPE TOWN

ISBN 0 86978 127 8

First Published 1958
Reprinted in this Edition 1969
Reprinted in this Edition 1971
Reprinted in this Edition 1973
Reprinted in this Edition 1976
Reprinted in this Edition 1979

ACKNOWLEDGEMENTS

I wish to thank "The Outspan" for permission to reprint the story in this book.

Also, thanks to Mr. S. Hendrikz of the Adelaide Free Press and Sister Ludwiga of King William's Town for their friendly help and encouragement.

Special thanks to Mr. J. Jackson for allowing me to use his illustrations.

CONTENTS

Iris Vaughan's diary	1
Maraisburg	4
Pearston	11
The Boer War	12
School	29
Edward 7	31
The gas light	33
Grahamstown	34
End of war	36
School Guy, Fox and Lancers	40
Poor school and the river and drift and eels	42
The Christian society and the circus	44
Fort Beaufort	48
Return to Adelaide	55

FOREWORD

by the

Editor of "Outspan,"

CHARLES BARRY

●

When Mrs. Niland submitted the manuscript of Iris Vaughan's Diary to "Outspan" for consideration, I thought it was one of two things—a clever hoax, or a major literary find.

There was never any doubt in my mind that the Diary was readable, immensely readable. But was it, in fact, the work of a young girl ?

We published a few instalments and waited for the public to react. We did not wait long. Letters poured in from delighted readers. And in these letters was the confirmation we were seeking. People from all over Southern Africa, who had not seen Iris Vaughan since childhood, remembered vividly the events she described. They also remembered that she spent much of her time writing a Diary.

Thus we were able to prove the Diary was genuine; and thus we were able to say confidently that it was a major literary find. I see no reason to change that view.

FOR IRIS VAUGHAN

"She was more than usual calm;
She did not give a singel dam."

Marjorie Fleming; 1803–1811.

Iris, the whole truth, nothing but the truth!
    Your Diry/Diray/Diery can recall
    Everyman's childhood: that enchanting scrawl
Evokes, with sorrel-sharpness, our own green youth,
That time before the last sad wisdom-tooth
    When we, too, knew our world Tom-Tiddler's-ground,
    And onion-pungent honesty was found
Blending with roses' high romance; and, sleuth
Of the savige, the sweet, the godforsaken Karroo,
    With your Sherlock eye, your Abou-ben-Adhem pen
    ("Write me as one that loves his fellow men"),
Who was among us, moving, noting – who?
    You, with your heart that knows without condemning,
    The peer of Daisy Ashford and Marjorie Fleming!

IRIS VAUGHAN'S DIARY

Today is my birthday. I am going to write a diry a diray a diery Book. Pop told me I could. He gave me this fat book. It was a govenment book, but it is mine now. I shall write here in the loft and hide my book in the old box with straw where no one can see it. Every one should have a diery. Becos life is too hard with the things one must say to be perlite and the things one must not say to lie. This is something I can never get right. If I say you are an ugly old man, that is bad manners, and if I say you are not an ugly old man I am telling a lie and not speaking the truth, the whole truth and nothing but the truth so help me God. That is what the peopel say in the witnes box when they are at a case in the courthouse. When they say this it a great

Iris.

sin to tell a lie. Pop says to the witnes who is to speak about the prisoner what you are to say is the truth the whole truth and nothing but the truth, and the witnes says so Help me God. Then he tells the truth and is not punished. But in our house it is not like that. The other day when Mr. O was eating with us he said You are my little sweethart, and I said NO and he said Why not and I said So help me God becos you are such an ugly old man with hair on your face. For what I was sent to bed without any more dinner even jelly and had a good jawing about perliteness. All the time I said I was only telling the truth Mom said Nonsense. you are just a rude little girl. So Pop said you have a diary and write all the truth in it and when you cant speak the truth its better to hold your tongue. That is why I am writing. Charles says it is all too much trubbel. Dont ever talk and you wont be

1

punished. But my tongue is unruly member Pop says and will cawse me to suffer much being a female.

Now I must tell about us. We are four children and Pop is the magistrat in this place called Maraisburg. It has one beautiful church which is Dutch we cant go to it becos we English Church. I said to Pop what is God English or Dutch and he said dont start that talk now you are too young to understand God is every kind of Church. There is one school and one shop and one hotel. It has one big dam. Here comes the water to wet the gardens. It comes in furrows down the streets. This place has no trees or rivers. Only sand and two hills and some milk bush becos it is the godforsaken Karroo. That is what Pop calls it.

Before we came here we lived in Cradock. It is a big town with a park and a railway train and a criket club. It is also a place where come many sick people called con sumtiffs who have a sickness of the lungs rotting of the lungs. Lots of them never get well. Pop is not a consumtiff. He comes from Wales the consumtiffs come from England. Pop is assistant magistrat. He is a very good criketer and was a captin. He played for the Gardens in cape Town and got silver medals which are fastened on his bats. He teaches us to play leg brakes keep your bat square, move

The photo—His sulks came in the photo.

2

your feet and play forward. He hits us when we dont listen. We started when we lived in Dundas Street in Cradock. Now we know it all. In Dundas street our house had a big pear tree and we had a foto taken under it. All had to wear the best clothes. Charles had his cross look becos he did not care to wear his best shoes they pinching him so madly. The foto taking man tried to make him laugh and said look at the canery bird coming out of the black foto taking box which stood on three sticks with a black cloth over his head. But charles just mad a worse look come on his face. He gets sulks. His sulks came out in the foto and spoilt it. Once he got bad sulks and walked in the water furrow with his best clothes on just before we went to a party. Mom was cross and locked him in the room. Then he kicked and screamed and we could not go to the party. Always I have to suffer for charles and his sulks. In Cradock were nice trees in the streets by the furrows. Here are no trees. In Cradock was a Slippery Rock where we have fun. Every afternoon Katryn takes us to the Rock. We climb to the top. In the middle of the rock, it is a very long great rock, is a lovely slippy footpath. You sit on top and someone pushes you and you sail away fast to the bottom just like a bird sailing in the air the wind blowing your hair and a strange noise in your ears like bees bussing. Mom made us take a bag to sit on becos we wore our drawers out sailing on our tails so much.

In Cradock we went to school at the Rektery with Miss Lucy. Her father is the preacher. They had a lovely garden with trees. One was a snowball. It had soft white snowball flowers and when they got faded Miss Lucy let us pick them and play with them. We had school in the garden and Canon Lew was always writing a sermon. When it is cold he is wrapped in a big rug round his legs and a cap to tie over his ears. He says it keeps me warm like a bug in a rug. I have never seen a bug in a rug. I asked Josef the fat constabel who took us to school what is a bug. J. said it is a thing like a big black louse and lives with dirty people and bites them. It has a strange smell I dont think Canon Lews looks much like a bug. I wanted to ask him but Miss Lucy never let us come near where he was writing, becos a worying him with too many kwestions.

Constabel used to take us every day to school. We took lemon syrup in bottles tied on with a cork and a string and some bath biskets to eat. Josef always had to hold my hand. He walks slow becos he is fat. Charles also walks slow, but he is not fat. He is just not wanting to go to school. I cant walk slowly. That is why Josef hold me tightly on my hand. He said Missie, I know you, you are the small skelm. You will run away round the corner into the market and I will not find you soon. I said Josef it is my feet that are skelm. They go by themselves, before I know. When it is so cold and so sunny and the wagons are all in the market and Cawoods shop full of peopel, my feet walk

3

slowly. They run before I know. Josef said it is your feet that run, but long before your eyes have looked where to run already.

After school we go to Pops offis. It is called a Court House. On the Court House floor is sore dust. To stop boots making a tramping noise when Pop is trying the cases. Mom says it is a filthy thing to have soredust, becos of all the spitting in the sore-dust. We go and sit inside Pop's bench which is like a big square box with a chair in the middle. There is a hole where his feet go and we clim in and peep through the cracks at the peopel sitting in the court while Pop is trying the prisoner. We often feel sorry for the prisoner when the polisman takes him away to jail. When we want to go to W.C. we pinch Pop on the leg and he says in a cross voice Constabel remove the children. The chief clark is Mister Stern. He comes from England. He is not a con sum-tiff. He gives us packets of fat jew jewbs sweets. Mr. Comish who is the first magistrat gives us a sixpens. Then we run to the chinaman shop and buy liquoris pipes and boot laces and sume-times butter skotch in tins with bunnies or dogs or birds on them. They called Calard and Bowsers and Mom says are the best sweets, better than sugar sticks or bulls eyes. Why Bullseyes They not looking like Bullseyes. I know becos I saw a bulls calf in the market and his eyes are not like bulls eyes sweets.

A great thing happened in Cradock. It was the laying of a foundashion stone. It will be the Victoria Horspital after the queen. Great many peopel came in the morning and stood round. It was near our house we saw all. It is in the veld. They sang and took lovely silver plates round for money, and a great flag (Pop called it Union Jack) was flying, and old peopel making long talks. Then they all went away. In the afternoon a great dust storm came. Everyone shut the houses, becos it blew every-thing away. But Pop and Charles and I ran to the stone becos the flag was blowing in the veld and all the silver plates flying in the air. We caught the silver plates and the flag and carried them home and Mom said. This is a dredful deed, Cecil. It is steeling. And Pop said Nonsense woman it is a gift from the elemense . . I said who is elemense. Pop said the wind. Mom used the silver plates to bake tarts in. She said they only tin. We will have tart tins for many years. The elemens gave us 24. Then we had to go to a new place Pop having the shift on. It called Maraisburg.

MARAISBURG.

Late when the sun was down we came in 2 postcarts to Marais-burg. It is a small place with two funny hills It looks as if the houses are against the hills but they are not. It is fenced in with a wire fence. To get in you must open a gate and close it again. Then you are in a Comonage. We stopped at the hotel. There

4

are no lamps in the street like in Cradock, so everywhere is dark. There is one glass lamp on a pole outside the Hotel with Hotel written on it. It is not a nice hotel. it is worse than at Pearston. The fllors are of mud. Every week the floors are smered with mis which is cowdung made soft like mud with water. It has a nasty smell. There is a room where men are sitting and laughing loudly and spitting into white basens on the floor. We got out of the carts and came inside. In the dining room are 3 tables and a big clock. At one table a man was eating and doing much belching and never excuse me please. We have only a candle to light the bedroom. Early in the morning we looked thro the window which is very small and opens with a hook. Klaas was brushing the horses in the yard. We helped him feed them He is going away again after breakfast and taking a traveler, he is the one who belches.

It has not been a nice going away this time in spite of nice long ride in postcarts becos our fox terier pup Gyp is lost all becos of Pop having a party befor we were going and coming home late at nite and getting sick and wanting to get out to throw up and leaving the door open. We were all sleeping on floor becos our beds had gone in the ox wagon long befor and Pop kicked pup and pup ran out and when we got up next morning Gyp was gone no gyp anywere and Mom said You see Cecil what your drinking party has done lost Gyp. We could not find him and postcarts may not wait. We all had to go and when we cried Pop said dont he has gone back to his mother and the post boy let us hold the reins if we stop crying and blew on his bugle loudly all thru the streets and Pop said he would get us a new pup soon.

On Monday Pop took us to the school with our bags. He left us at the door with a big girl. She took us through a small passige where all the hats hang. She hangs ours there too girls on one side and boys on other side. Boys wear caps. Then we went

Charles—was getting his sulky look.

5

in the Masters room. Here were lots of children. The master sat on a high place at the top of the room. We had to go up 3 stips to speak to him. All were still and looking at us. Charles was getting his sulky face so I held him tight by the hand. He does not like school clothes. He said his collar was scraping his neck and his shoes were hurting his toes and his trousers too tight round hisstomick. We know this school can never be like Mis Lucys. Here is a strange fear feeling for us. The girl said Mister de Ry here are 2 new children. Mr. de Ry stood up. He had black clothes on and was long and very thin and also his face had many crinkles in it. He said now I must write your perticlers. What are perticlers I wonder. Then he said what is your name and I said Iris Vaughan. He said is that all your names and I had to say the other names which I hate Emily and Henriette and Charles would not say at all becos of his sulks. I said Charles Theodore, becos he hates Theodore like I hate Emily but we are being called after our granmother and granfathers. Then the master said where were you born and I said in a desert. He said dont talk nonsense child, where were you born. I said I was born in the desert and Charles in a tent. He said what desert. I said I dont know what desert. He said can you read. I said Yes. He said Take them to Miss Annie. We went to another room. Miss Annie was small and pretty. She said Have you got a slate. I said yes and she put me in a long desk next to another girl with a very long nose. Her name is Martha. She tried to take Charles to sit at a small table with 3 other boys. But Charles held to my hand and when she tugged at him he opened his mouth and roared like he does when he is cross. It was sich a terribel roar that Miss Annie let him sit with me. She said Can you read, what can you read. I said Scotts Tales and Dickens and Lambs Tails of Shakespier. Miss Annie looked at me a long time. Then she said can you write. I said yes. She said take this chalk and write on the Board. I wrote A Bird sings sweetly. She said you better go in standard 1. But I cant do the sums so I must go with the babies for sums which is a dusgrace for me. When I take out my slate and my small bottel of water and sponge to clean my slate all the children giggel. I see that they have only a wet rag to clean. Some just spit on their slates. I do not like this school. At lunch time all the girls are skipping and talking and looking at my shoes and white socks. Many have no shoes or socks. At 12 o'clock we are let out. I run fast to the hotel. Mom says did you like it. I say No and then I start to be sick. Pop says it is becos it is strange. It will be better next week. That night I cried in my pillow for Miss Lucy nice school. How will it get better this terribel school with no snowball trees and books and Canon, only hard benches and spitting on slates.

We walked with Pop to look at Mburg. It has a market square and 2 shops oosthuizens and Billinhams. There is also a big sloot at the back side of houses which has no water except when

He opened his mouth and roared.

it rains. There are big houses with gardens they are calling them water erfs becos they only ones getting watter in a furrow from the big dam at top of the street. We all went to look at this dam. It has a strong wall Pop says a good thing becos if it broke we would all be dead. The wall has a road on top. Pops offis is small but they are making a nice new one for him here. Constable is George he comes from King willems town. He speaks good english pop says.

The most wonderful thing is to happen to us. A piano is coming today on the oxwagons from Cradock. Today we watched it being lifted off the wagon. It is in a big wooden box. Six boys had to pick it up. It took weeks to come from Cape Town first in the train and then in the transport. Mom opened it and sat down in front of it and made music. Then Pop sang 2 songs one after another I stood on the Bridge at midnight and Sweet Alice Ben Bolt, and all the servants Meisjie and Willem and us all stood round and listened and Willem said it was regte mooi.

After supper we all came close round the piano and sang out of the Globe Song Book, Granfather's clock and Juanita and Soldiers Farewell and Pop sang down by the River side I straid and my Josefine all about napolens wife and Mom played lots of tunes and then we all sang God save the queen and went to bed. It was wonderful having our own Piano at last. The ox wagons brought us oranges too. Every year at this time they come full up with bags of oranges and everyone runs to buy. It is the only time we ever see oranges. Mom bought 2 bags and divided one out between us, each one to get a share. I must hide mine in a safe place from Charles becos he eats his and then he eats mine and Florences. We roll them soft with our foot, then poke a hole and suck all the juice. Then we eat all that is left. This eating of peel gives me a pain in my stumuck, but not Charles. He is lucky to not have a weak stomick. The wagons all span out at the outspan place. The drivers chase the oxen to the dam to drink water then let them eat on the comonage. Then they colect sticks and cow-dung and make fires to cook their kettle and keep them warm for at night it is so cold that the water gets hard ice on it On the road your boots slip where it is wet and you fall. Sometimes it snows. When the drivers are drinking their coffee we talk to them. They tell us where the oranges grow trees with shiney leaves and thorns, and oranges hanging like golden balls. Some day I will see them too.

Where the outspan place is are many spiders. The babiaan spinneskops with long brown hair on them. Never do we walk in the veld without boots becos of many scorpeons and other spiders. There are also the piogters, black with white stripes when you touch them they shoot nasty burning stuff in your eyes. There are tok tokkies. They are the knocking kind beetle. One day I had two toks in my room and Charles had 2 in his room. In the night when all was asleep the toks got out and started to walk, the wives looking for the husbands which were mixed up. The wives have a brown spot on their stumick. When they cant find them the husbands stands still and knock with his stumick on the ground and the wives knock back. That night they knocked so loud on the floor Mom woke up and said Cecil, wake up someone is knocking, and Pop got up and looked at the back door and at the front but no one was there. Then he went to bed and said Patty you dreaming and blew out the candle. When all was quiet the toks knocked again and Mom said whose dreaming now, and Pop said someone is playing the fool and he went to back door and Mom went to front but no one. Mom said this house is haunted. Pop said Rot and Mom said Mrs. Oost told me and old woman died of hunger in this house when her peopel went to nagmaal and forgot her. Pop said old woman be dammed, ghosts dont knock. But the toks went on knocking and Pop said Iris and Charles are you making this noise, becos if you dont stop I'll tan your bottoms for you. Then we all sat quiet to listen and Charles said "It is only the toks look there they are behind the door, and we saw them knocking loudly with their stomachs on the floor Pop said, My God, who would have guessed these dam beetles knew about morse code in their secks life. Then he threw them out and we all went to sleep.

8

Pop has bought us a new dog. Not a pup it is a pointer. Pop likes many dogs. he also like fowls and horses and carts and criket. He liked football but he broke his leg at Gardens and had to come home in a weel barrow now he only plays criket. Mom says all these things cost to much money. Pointer is called Ponta. Pointer dogs are good for hunting They also get many pups to make money if you sell them. Pop said now we will see the fine hunting with Ponta becos Ponta is trained and will point out the birds in the veld. We went in the dog cart to hunt. Pop sat in front with me and Charles and we held Ponta tied fast. Then we outspaned and walked letting Ponta run in front to show birds and Ponta ran a lot smelling for birds and Pop had his 3 A in the gun for shooting and then Ponta did a strange thing. He stopped and held his head strait and his tail straita and Pop said no sound he sees abird. Then we came near but no korhan ran up to fly and when Pop came to Ponta he swore loudly becos Ponta was pointing at a tok tok beetle and we laughed becos of Ponta seeing tok not bird but never again did Ponta go to hunt with us. He stays in a kennel in the yard and is a watch dog. Then Pop got a pure breed pointer from Gramstown a lady dog who will have much pups.

Here in Mb. we burn a strange kind of coal. It is dung. The farmer brings it in his wagon every month. In big squares. It is sheeps and goats dung tramped fast and dug out. We saw it at Vermaaks farm. It is called mis. Here are also salt pans on Ogilvies farm. It is wonderful to see salt scratched out of the ground. They have big dams full of water. Then after a long time it gets hard on top and it is salt, and the boys go with long planks and scrape the salt and makes heeps of it. hard and white like snow. We put sticks and things in and when we fetch them they are hard and pretty with salt. Also on Mr. Os farm are many springboks. Pop will take us to see a spring bok hunt. Here is also a big hole where they make the bricks to build houses. In this big hole live many great frogs called bull frogs, becos they bellow like a bull. Once we were bringing a buul frog home but Mom was in the yard and saw us and said No this I cannot bear and we had to take bull frog back. Ogilvie has a boy who comes on a horse to get the post in a bag. His name is Tonio. Pop says from Italy. He lets us ride his horse and tells us many funny poems and once Charles said this funny poem about the old lady who rides on the tiger to Pop and he got savage and said this is not the poems you must say. Now Tonio tells us no more funny poems. We went to the spring bok hunt. We will not go again becos of being in the line of fire. Many shooters went to and spanned out their carts and we too and Pop put us with Willem away to wait and all the shooters rode away and when the boys drove the springboks for them to shoot at and the springboks turned and came by us and the shooters forgot about us and were shooting the boks and Willem pushed us flat on ground and said le stil nou and we heard the bullets and then the spring boks were

9

Pop came fast on his horse.

past and many were lying on the ground shot and Pop came fast on his horse and said My God are you alive. Then we made a fire and had a picnic but Mom was savige with Pop and said never again Cecil.

When we were in Cradock we once got a shift on to Pearston in a train. Mom wasnt liking it becos it was karoo. I said what is Karoo Pop and he said a land of sweet bludy all Mom said do not speak to child like that Cecil. The train was wonderful like riding in a little house with 2 flat seats each side and 2 up bunks over them. Charles and I sleep in the up bunk and all the luggige. Pop had a plan to be hiding me under the rug when the ticket man came and not pay becos he said it pleased him to do Govement out of one pound they doing him out of much else but Mom said Cecil for the keeper of the law you the worst man. Then Mom got out the baskets and food and tea in bottels and rolled in thick newspaper and we had chiken and bread and Pop had brandy out of a flask. These kinds of trains Pop says are called dogboxes becos you may not walk from one box to another except when it is standing still then you get off on a step. When we got to Hanover road in was nite. We had to get out. it was very cold and snow was wanting to fall. nowhere to sit becos the train was gone and we must wait for the next. My teeth where chatering with the cold So Pop put Charles and me between the big bales of wool and covered us with rug and then it got better. Poor sheep without wool in this cold veld I said. I have never seen a sheep without wool, is its teeth chatering and Pop said if they had not cut off its wool your teeth will still be chatering be thankful, then a man came, and said we must all come in his office and sit by the coal fire and we warmed so much we took coat and mufler off and got nice hot coffee to drink.

PEARSTON

Pearston is a very small place. It has a river but no water in. We live in hotel. It is a bad one. It has earth floors The one night we were sleeping Charles said look at the thing coming out of a hole in corner by the lamp, and Mom said Snake and screeched to some one to bring a stick but the snake got a frite and went in the hole again. The hotelman came out and put a saucer

Hans.

of milk by the hole and a boy Hans sat by the hole with a stick and all were very quiet and then again the snake came out slowly waving his head about. When it was rite out Hans hit it and killed it. It was a big one and might have crept to Florence cot beside the lamp and bitten her. Now the hole is closed. Hans says snakes like milk and sometimes drink milk out of cows. We have not yet seen a cow milking. Hans showed us milk out of cows when he drove the 2 cows home. Cows have it hard to live at P. becos there is not good grass for them to eat. This is prickley pear land and babbons in the mountains. We rode today in a basket carage It is Mrs. Oharas. She is the wife of Dr. and she sent her carage and pony and boy to take us for a drive becos

11

we asked. All the way we rode we waved our hands and shouted this is Mrs. Oharas basket cart and she letting us drive and Mom came out of the hotel and stopped the boy and said if this is the way you behaving no more ride. Then we were quiet and Mrs. OH gave us cake and milk when we came back and said I am glad you like my basket my dears. Then we went to stay at an hotel in the mountain called Brunties Hogte becos it is better for children. Pop came on a horse on Sunday to see us. Here it is very wild. We see the babons on the rocks making a strange noise like barking. The Mother B. carry the baby B. on there backs and the fathers always walk behind to see they are safe. We must never go away from house becos babons are savige and steal you. Hans is a korrel kop bushman. We are now in the mud hotel again becos we must go back to Cradock. A great rain came in the nite and rained all day and then Pop came and said put on your coats and come fast to the river. No one can cross it. it is a flood a terribul site the water all yellow and dirty and making awful noise and throwing dead trees and dead sheep and donkeys up and down which are dead. On the other side was Hans sitting with the 2 cows he could not get across and was wet and cold and I cried and said Pop cant God help poor Hans to get across on this side and be warm and Pop said God has helped Hans that he did not cross in the river when the flood came down or he would be dead. he wil go and wait under a bush with his cows and when the water is low and then come. The next morning Hans was in the yards with the 2 cows when we woke up. He said I have seen many greater floods I was not afraid to sleep under the bush. I milked the cows out that they would not burst. Hans told us lots of stories about Oom leu and jackals and Haasie and the fat melting out of his tail and fossie. Hans has lived many years and knows much. I like Hans. Then we came back to Cradock. On the staton the first man we saw was the water closet man. He empties the bukets. we were very glad to see him. We went to stay with Miss Diger until the house is ready.

THE BOER WAR

Yesterday the first Boers came. We looked at the milk bushes near the brick fields and saw the men on horses bobing and riding from one side to the great sloot on the other. Charles said, Pop lots of farmers are riding near the bricks. Pop was reading his new book about Minie haha Hiawatha laughing water and would not listen. Then the next thing lots of men were riding in the street and Willem ran and said "Seer dit is de Boers and Pop said My God so they are and then the Boers were opening the gate.

12

They came in a long line making a great dust (Boer War).

They nearly all had beards like men in the Bible. They took Pop away in his slippers and no hat. Mom ran after him and said heres your cap can I bring your boots He said to hell with boots look after the safe keys.

We sat on the wall and saw the Boers riding all over. Charles said they have taken all the polis horses and now they are taking Sarjent. Sarjint saw us sitting on the wall and said go inside youngsters. But we didnt go we wanted to see what Boers did. Then came the man on the white horse. He had a band of bullets round his chest and holding his gun on his knee in the air. He came inside the gate and said "where did your father leave his keys." We all jumped off the wall fast and ran inside to hide. Florence and I hid in the closet. Charles lay flat in the manger. The Boer saw Charles and said "where is your horse we know you have a horse. Charles said I dont know. We all knew Pop had locked it up in the feemale cell in the jail. Pop said if Naughty holds his mouth and you all hold yours they wont find him. We all shut our mouths and even though the man asked us twice and we were trembling. Willem said Boers stab peopel with sharp knives called baynets. We did not see any baynet with this Boer. Then Mom came back and said "leave the children. Here are the safe keys. there is no money." Then we trembled again. All the money lots of it was tied up in the tops of the curtains in the dining room. The Boer was standing right beside the curtain. We all knew not to look at the curtains. But what if it fell suddenly down at his feet. What would he do to Mom and us. The other Boers came in the room. They took the tomatoes off the supper table. Then they all went away again. Mom went away and Sanna our cook willems wife took us to the square to see what they were doing to Pop. It was getting dark in the square. Pop was standing with Sargint and two kafir polismen and Boers were standing behind him with guns. We began to cry. Then the Boer on the white horse took off his hat and spoke a long pray. Then they sang. We thought it was Rule Brittania but Sanna said it was a salm singing. Then they took Pop and Sargint into the offis and the others broke open the shop doors and threw out everything to eat and to wear. It was very dark and Sanna said "huis toe." We ran home and sat in the dark. Then Mom came and was talking with Willem. They lit a candle and went in the bedroom and pulled down the blind. She wrote a note on a small piece of paper. Willem opened his shoe at the bottom and put it in there. Then he ate his supper and ran away. Mom said the man on the white horse broke the telegarf machime before Mrs. Oost could send a message. He hit it with his gun. Willem is running to Cradock Sanna said He will tell the soldaats. If they catch him the Boers will shoot him, but they wont catch that skelm. It was late when they let Pop come home and sleep. They went away early in the morning like the wind with all the horses but not Naughty. Pop says one day they will get him luck cant last forever. Today the soldaats came becos Willem got to Cradock. The Majer rode up to the gate just like the Boers, only he had smart clothes with shining buttons and polish on his boots and belt and Pop was digging round the peach trees, and the Majer didn't think he was a magistrar and shouted at him, "Hoist the flag, hoist the flag" and pointed at the flag pole and Pop was in a bad temper becos it was hot with so much digging and he stood up and looked at the Majer with a savige look and said "Bloody well hoist it yourself. Up one day down the next . . . if you would move faster it might stay up longer." Then we saw the militery had come, but not like the Boers came bobbing up and down on the veld and milk bushes. They came in a long line making a great dust with canons and things to make a camp at the back of the house. Then we put up the flag. Pop calls them the colums. Many colums come now to camp round us, with lots of tents and bugle blowings and horse pikets and lots of sentries to shout "Who goes there" Then you say Friend and he says "Advance friend and give the counter sign and you advance and say the word. It was Miranda after the Majors wife, but Pop said "wife my eye." Why my eye? and then the sentry says "Pass friend." If you dont know the word you get taken to the offiser on guard and he locks you up in a guard tent. Our friend Bartelman, the Majers batman told me all this and explained the strange things

colums do. He gave me his choclate. Since the Boers broke all
the shops we never get sweets any more. The Tommies get sweet
choclate from the Queen and give us some. They feel sorry for us
becos we the only English children here. Never do we get butter
or sugar any more. We eat dry beans and fat on our bread. I
hate fat it sticks in my teeth. Sometimes we get golden syrup.
Mom puts it on the stove. It gets soft and runny and is much
more.

Every nite george comes to teach us. We sit in the kitchen and
he shows me how to do sums and parsing and helps Charles becos
he knows little. When we finish Mom gives us coco to drink.
George is the best constabel we have had. He is a very clever boy.
Sometimes he sings for us little brown jug how I love the.

Today a new colum has come. It is called the D.M.R.'s and
the CMR's and the PAG's. Majer Grant came with them. Also
Leftenant Feeld and many other ofisers. They all came to our
house to have baths. Sanna was makking the hot water all day.
Tonight a new thing is going on. Everyone maust be putting out
the lights. Pop was savige. He said "a lot of dam rot these militery think of." He had to go to bed in the dark becos the blind
was thin and sentries walking in the streets to catch you and he hit
his toe on the bed and said awful cursings all about the militery.
The other night we heard shots. We thought it was a battle. It
was only one of the sentries thought he heard something. But it
was dark and he did not look well. Pop said today that what he
did not see well was a man called Smuts and his 59 Boers going
over the dam wall to Cradock. Pop says it is all this silly pass
friend and sentry go businness taking up so much time. Boers
dont have that and they never get caught. They always see the
colums miles away and then come after and pick up all the bullets
and guns and tired horses the colums leave behind. What a disgrace Pop says. I think so too. Now the Boers have taken
Naughty and my horse with the mange which militery left and
Charles also. Today we heard we are going to get a shift on to a
place called Adelaide. It is on a river and has trees. Fancy
trees. Here we have only Karoo bushes and a big dam and
springboks and korhaan and asvogels and the dustdevils making
long curly chimneys in the sky when it is hot. Now we will have
water running all the time over stones. Charles says we will catch
fish and learn to swim . . .

Pop went to C. Town and wired to say we must leave at once.
We went in a mule wagon and the pointer dogs too. When we
were going out of Mbg Willem said here is a kaki. The Tommy
rode fast up to us and said what place is this. Mom said It is
Mburg. my isn't it Tebus he said Mom said No its not we are
goint to Tebus now. it is Mburg." "And a dam dangerous spot it
is. I've lost my colum and my horse is done and you must take me
with you or I shall be a prisoner." Willem said Nee if we meet
Boers and you with us they will stop us and shoot me. Tommy

15

said if you not taking me they will catch me and shoot me. At last Mom sat him between us at back and I pray they may not find him and shoot or stab with baynet like Bartelman showed us. When we came to Tebus Pop was there. He saw the Tommy sitting with us and was savige he said damn you could have got my family into danger sitting there you selfish—he said an awful word and tommy said sorry sir where is Gatacers colum where I belong." "It is in stansburg. go and stay where you belong you deserving to be shot." Then the train came in.

Florence never saw a train She and Bell the pointer dog fell over backwards with frite. It was a new sort of train with a passige and wash basen. At 5 o'clock men climbed on the roof and pushed the lamps in the holes to lite. They look like round plates and had green shades over on wire rings to make it dark when you sleep. Charles slept on top bunk and pulled it open all night. Mom was cross. Then the train brought us to Cookhouse. Here we had to get out. Why is it called this funny name. I asked everyone, for there were many Tommies here. One said becos it was once a place for cooking, and one said it was becos it was so dam hot you always feel cooking here. Then I asked Pop and he said "stop asking questions. you are a nuisance." There are only prickly pears growing at this Cookhouse millions of them. We have to stay here two days and I think the man who said it was a hot place is right. The military commandered the 2 Cape carts which Pop had hired to take us to Bedford, for there is no train here. Pop was in a savige mood and swore all the time having to sit in this hot Cookhouse. The Hotel is full of military who have all the rooms. We all slept in one big room 2 in one bed. Florence bit me on the arm becos I kicked her and she fell on the floor. Then we both got punished. Being the eldest is a hard life. you the one gets all the jawings and Mom says if she staying longer in this place she will be a loonatick. What is a loonatick.

Then we came to Bedford. We came in a big cart called a BUZZ. It was an old buzz used once for driving peopel to Grahamstown to the train. Its a nice kind of wagon. It had 4 horses to pull us all. It also had lots of bugs. When it got hot the bugs ran out the tent. Charles and I saw them first sitting in the back seat of the Buzz. We had a race seeing who could kill the most squeezing them and not making one sound. That was a mistake. Pop said "Why are those devils so quiet at the back seat." He was sitting in the front with Mom. We said "we not doing anything only killing the many bugs." and the row he made all of a sudden about the bugs. And Mom screeching and stopping the Buzz and all had to get out and the driver said "Bass dit is maar tampans." They were not proper bugs like Canons bug in a rug eating people. They only ate on fowls, the driver said. Even this did not please Mom and Pop. Old peopel are strange in their ways. The driver said the buzz had been kept beside a fowl hok it being very old and military not want-

16

ing it, and the fowls used to often sleep in the buzz and left the bugs behind ...

Bedford has a nice hotel. A doubel storey called Robinsons. Pop went to talk to the militery about taking his carts and the bugs. A nice old man like father Xmas came to talk. He is the father of the leftenant who had baths with us. He lives here. He saw us all looking in the shop window where are many sweets. He said why are you standing there so long. We said we have not seen so many sweets for years. He said God bless my soul and gave us each a whole shilling. A whole silver shilling. Before we only get a penny. We ran inside and took a long time to buy all the ones we wanted. I bought likerice boot laces which last a long time. I can roll them up and keep them in my jelly bag cap where Charles cant get them to eat. Florence bought canon balls, and

Pop had his savage look.

one canon ball stuck in her mouth It was an awful thing to get it our again and her face getting so red. Mom was nearly crying and Pop so savige. And that night I had a billious attac becos of my waek stumick. I had eaten the least bootlaces of all. It isnt fair to have a stumick like mine. Charles eats hundreds and never gets sick.

We came to Adelaide in the 2 Cape carts Pop got back from the militery. Charles and I and the portmantoes came in the one. The driver told us about a little child called Andy who lived before we were born in the mountains of Adelaide. His father was a parson and one Sunday when the parson was having church and leaving his little child behind, the Kafirs stole the child away and hid him in a cave. And the peopel thought it was baboons stealing the child. But the Kafir who was cross with the parson killed him and left him in the cave and only many years after did they find the bones of the poor little child and knew what had

17

happaned. In this place we will see many kafirs called REDS becos they wear red clay bankets and beads. The driver says we must go on the other side of Adelaide to a place called KING where the Kafirs live always in the red blankets and carry long sticks called Kirries to fight with. They are quite tame not fighting like long ago.

We came over a great red bridge into Adelaide. The river had great trees hanging in the water. It is the Koonap. We saw the Dutch Church pop says it is looking like westmister abby with a big stone tower. We passed Mr. Goldis shop a fine shop with the house joined on it. It has shining green bowls and red hanging on chains on the veranda. There is a daddy goldi with a soft white beard like Eli in Bible and lots of other Mr. Goldis and 3 lovle Miss Golds really lovely called Hetty and Fanny and Charlot. Fanny is the best. In the town is a square. In the square are 2 hotels Migleys a small flat one and Longs a great doubel story. We living in Mr. Longs. This is fun with banisters. Pop says one of you devils sail on this banister and you know what to get. On the top is a balconi. It is easy to drop water or bits of gravel on peopels head below. But Pop knew we were thinking that. Some-

Hit a man coming out of the Brandy Shop (Bar).

18

times he knows things quite well. He said "The first one who drops even one spit will have the penny pocket money taken away for 8 weeks." We wont drop anything, becos when he looks like that he always does it.

The peopel who keep the hotel are Mr. Bob and Mrs. Bob. They have 3 girls Ivy Gladys and Mabel. Gladys is old as me and has 2 nice long black plaits and wears brown canvas shoes Mabel weers boots. Ivy has gold hair. There are some boys Jack is nearly old and Olly is like Charles. They have the many couzens Hollamby Armstrong Davis and Jim Longs who have not a mother. There sister Florry looks after them. Mrs. Bob has the nicest face and is always laughing. I dont think she ever getting cross. Mr. Bob and Pop talk every night and much laughing Nellie helps her with the house keep she is fat Jack sells the brandy. Yesterday Charles came down the banister with no

Paul.

one looking and hit a man coming out of the brandy shop. The door of the brandy shop is by the stairs it is called BAR why bar why not brandy or wine. No one will tell me this. the man fell over, Charles said he was a kind man he only said you be more careful next time. His name is Mort he paints houses and has a very long thin hanging mustach. Hills shop is opposit. Mr. Hill is bald and fattish. He has a girl Evie and a boy Paul with curls like Lord Faunleroy. Charles says if Mom made him to wear curls like Lord F. he would hate her for ever and cut them off. They have couzens he is Dr. Jock. They are Scots. On Sunday Bill and Dudley wear the kilt. Margy is there sister and has much frizzie hair and nice clothes. In Hills show room is a small lady Elfie she looks like one of the elfs in Hans Anderson. She is very nice to buy from. Here the militery dont come in colums like Mb. A few come just sort of in and out to cause much troubel

19

pop says. All get excited when they think Boers might come. They never come here anyway we dont mind becos they used to us. They much like Pops and oncles not stabing children with baynets like Willem said. Not even when they got naughty and Charles and my horses in jail Pop says never can we have horses again for who will pay the compensasion money. Anyway we have got a river instead.

We have all been to fish with Jocks and Hills and mothers and fathers and took our tea. All carried. We went to first krans. It is close to the houses. Second krans is far away. They have lots of great trees and rocks and river and grass. Worms are dug out of the mud for bate and pulled on a hook. We had bent pins. I do not like to fish pushing the poor worms on the hook and puling up poor fish with a hook in the mouth. This is tortur. They jump about a long time before they are dying. You have to gut them. When I wanted to get sick Charles said you wont get sick when you eating them. Which is true Why does so many nice things be killed for us to eat. I wish it was diferent. The big boys swim in a hole called Deep hole becos it has no bottom. Only very good swimmers and others swim there.

The militery are also here but not as many as in Maraisburg but no Boers. Only a few militery and no colums, but a town Guard in case a few Boers come at night. Everyone gets excited when they hear Boers might come. But we seen so many Boers we dont mind. We get excited about the river and the trees willows and little stone and soft sand. I never knew it could be so wonderful to walk in water with no red mud in your toes. We swing on the willow trees. Pop says they have long branches and are called Weeping Willows. Like in the song he sings at night "Fair fair with golden hair sang the poor mother while weeping, under the willow shes lade with care, under the willow shes sleeping." No fair is sleeping under these willows. We caught some mulletfish and ate it at breakfast I dont like much to eat this fish. It is all spitting out and little putting in becos of so many bones. In the end I just eat bread and jam. Florence got a bone in her throte and there was an awful hitting on the back and doing things to get it out.

Now we live in a house called semy detashed. We have half Miss Calagans have half. All have the one yard. We never rember to keep out of Miss Calag half. Opposit lives Mrs. Singer and a pretty daugter called Maud she plays the organ in Church. Here lives also the Davis with no father only a mother called Granny Davis becos she is nursing sick peopel. Benny and Pearl live next to them. Mr. Ben is a tailor. He has a long brown beard and walks very slowly to work. Benny is long and thin: All are in our class at school. The man who has the school is Mr. Donald. They call him Jonny Bok becos he has a beard like a goat. He has a brother who has a shop which has strange windows with rolling iron shuters on them so that no one can rob. He has many children Simon and Josey and Connie and Mona and Matt and Martin. Miss Queeny Sparks is teaching st. 4. She is fierce you dont make a noise with her. Mr. Hanekom is teacher in big children. He is more fierce. I am afraid of him Miss Rena Sparks is pupel teacher and she is the nicest and kindest of all. When Jonny Bok looks at you you think quickly what have I done wrong now. We have an awful class here. It is a DOH rey me singing. Never shall I get this right.

Here is an English Church. This is the first time we will go to Church and really learn about God. In Maraisburg was only the Dutch church and we did not learn about God. Only sometimes Pop read us out of the Childs Bible about Moses and David and other old men. All had beards. Solomon was the wisest becos he had so many wives and learnt to keep alive for 200 years. That was becos God liked him. I asked Pop why he does not have many wives and he said God forbid, and told me not to ask silly questions. This Church has a choir where singing peopel sit. They have to bellow very loudly to help all the other peopel who sit in the benches to sing strange songs called salms and chant. Not easy to do, becos sometimes they go so fast you cant get your breath and then so slow you far in front of everyone of the choir. I would not like to sit in that choir, becos of everyone looking at you. if your garter came down you would have great troubel to get it up with all staring. We have all got the red prayer books. We look in them but dont know what it is all about. Charles has best seat by the window and is putting his name on it with a knife.

The parsons name is Damp. He is young but bald. He has not a wife he is a bacheldor and comes often to our house. He is very strange sometimes. Charles says he is not right, but Hester our cook, says who is not right, all have a little mad in them. Mom says no one would think Pop was a parson's son with his savige temper and his swearing. He does not swear when Mr. Damp comes. Mr. Damp says he is going to make Christians of us. He says you all little heathens not knowing about God and Church. You will go to Sunday school." I said "what is Sunday school and he said it is the nicest place. The next day he brought a game called Spilikens. A game Chinaman play, a truly horofic game. Thin little ivory sticks like birds or fishes, you throw on the table then you have a picker up stick and have to hook them out without moving even one. We had to sit round the table in the afternoon to play this with him. It was awful. I got the cramp in my leg with sitting still so long. Our hands began to shake and then Florence pinched Charles when he was picking up her spiliken bird and he said a loud swear word like Pop and there was a bad time for all of us then. But Charles said it was better to have a punishing then to sit there any more. So we went outside and walked on Miss Callagans wall and she gave us a bisket. We have been to Sunday school. I can see we will suffer for our religion like the Children of Isrel in the desert. Becos we have

21

been so long without Church we must learn all now fast. Only Charles and I go to S. school. Florence is still too small. We go at 2 when it is very hot and all old peopel sleep. Round the Church is a green hedge with large lovely cherries on it, Gladys Long said they are Kei apples and not poison. I said is it allowed for us to pick them. She said yes but no one likes to eat Kei apples. What a strange thing that no one wants to eat them. I et 1 and Charles et 3 and then we went into Sunday S. Mr. Damp teaches the boys and Miss Jolly the girls. Miss Jolly is the one who bellows loudest in the choir. They all said long verses out of the Bible and knew things about collects and salms. Everything they asked I didnt know. Mr. Damp came to listen and said "they proper heathens I must take them in hand." I got red with shame. When I have children the first thing I will teach them is out of the pray book. I wanted to tell him I knew about Moses and Aaron and Solomon but I got a sudden awful sick feeling in my stummick and knew I was going to vomit. Charles

He has to sing in the Choir.

also had the feeling. I just pushed quickly over Gladys and ran out. Miss Jolly tried to stop me, but I ducked. Charles and I got out together. It was the Ky apples. They make all peopel to vomit. I had to go to bed becos of my weak stumick. Mr. Damp came after S. School and said their behavir was out rageuos. I said "Mr. Damp have you ever et of Ky apples then you will know what they do they make you to throw up. One must not throw up in a Church." Mom said "Be quiet at once." Old people are never fair when you try to explain.

Charles is in a fury. He has to sing in the CHOIR. How terribel He ran and kicked the door with savige rage and is hating Mr. Damp with a terribel hating. I am glad for once I am a girl. On the top of the Dutch Church tower is a pompom gun to protect us when the Boers come. Charles dont think one pompom can do much good, because all the Maxims and other canons the colum

had at Maraisburg never stopped one Boer. They could not stop
that man Smuts and his 59 Boers with no pompoms, running over
the dam wall. Pop says the Boers are the best Gorillers for fighting ever known. Why Gorillers? Gorillers are big apes. Pop
says Goriller fighting is when they run round and never get caught.
Smuts is the leading Goriller running from the Transvaal right
down to here. With the pompom on the Tower sit some soldiers,
town guards, all day and all night in case the gorillers come, and
tonight the other Town Guards must go out and sleep in a trench
with some stones in front of it. They must take guns for shooting
and a blanket. Pop took some brandy in a flask becos of the cold.
Pop and Dr. Jock caught the lumbago staying in the trench and not
one goriller. Pop says it is a lot of bloody rot. They should all
build block houses with barb wire round like at Tebus. Up in
the tower sits a gun crew. The chief of them is a nice man called
Piet. His mother lives next to us. Pop says Piet is a good soldier.
He keeps himself and the crew awake at night with the playing of
poker. At first I thought it was a thing for poking in the fire now
I know it is a kind of card game like Vreetens. Piet is the best
poker player in the place. Early in the morning when it was
getting light the pompom started to fire. We all ran out in pajamas. Pop climbed in the big peper tree to see what Piet was shot-
ting at. We all climbed in peper trees except Mom. She said
Cecil come down at once and tell me if we must hide the money
again. Nothing hapened with all the shooting, only Pop tore his
trousers a big hole in them and said savigely that Piet was just doing that to make all jump out of their beds in the bitter cold. Mom
said I know better he was having a good night with the bottle and
thought he saw Gorillers when all he saw was the town guard
coming home before time.

Charles hates the Choir practis. In Church they wear long black
dressing gowns with white shirts hanging over them and walk in
front of Mr. Damp two and two like the elephant and the Kang-
aroo in the story book. Charles trying every Friday when it is the
practis to tell Pop that he hates choirs but Pop now thinks the
Church is wonderful and is a warden man taking round the plate
for the money. After all this time of living nicely like the Children
of Israel in the wilderness we have to make up for it and go to
Church two times every Sunday. Sunday is the only day I dont
like in Adelaide. I wonder if God likes Sunday School. I asked
Mr. Damp and he gave me a good rowing. This week Charles was
cast out of the Choir. Mr. Damp said there was something wrong
with his voice and he was naughty. Charles said he made his
voice wrong like that on purpose becos Ollie told him that was
the way to get out of the Choir. Charles was so glad he gave me
one of his blood ally marbles.

We are now going to a new house, which is next to the Court
House. It is much bigger and better than Miss Calagans. Once
before the war it was the Bank. One side of our house has 2 big

rooms. Here a lawyer man called Hendriks works. He is soon marrying with a lady who looks like one of the 7 princeses in Grimms she is tall and beautiful. Our part of the house has lots of rooms and stoeps and passiges. It was filthy becos of the militry having it. All the ceelings are made of rag and Mom had to paint them brown to hide the dirt. An awful thing happened to Coot and me. In the one side of the long passige is a small dark room with a strong thick door. It was called the strong room for the bank Pop said. Here they kept all the pounds and tresures. We went to look in there in case one pound got left behind. Then Florence shut the door and ran away and we could not open it. Coot screamed and I beat on the door with my shoe. The dark same tighter and tighter and Coot held on my legs. She is only small and noises came in my ears and then Charles opened the door and I fell on the floor and Mom had to get Doctor Jock. He said it was only a strange kind of thing becos of being closed in a black space which made me to fall dawn. Now the door is locked and the key is hidden away.

At the back of the house is a very great yard with big blue gum trees. At the very back are the old stables. Mr. Armer has a cofin shop there. We climb over a high gate and go in to see Sam Brown making cofins. We pick up the long curls of wood he calls them shavins and bring them home to put on the fire. Cofins are pretty things. When they are ready they are covered with white cloth and black cloth and sometimes with painting. Some cost lots of money.

Behind our yard is anoth house with only one big blue gum. It is the biggest tree in Adelaide. One day a policeman was standing under it. The lightning came and struck the tree and killed him and burnt his shirt off and burnt a picture of the whole tree on his chest. Why did it do that. The Lightning also struck Mrs. Donald Evies mother She was carrying baby Mona and it melted the gold chain round her neck and knocked the nails out of her boot. They were not killed like the Policeman only got sick from the lightning strike. Simon Donald works in Pops office. He writes on a thing we have never seen befor. It is called typewriter. He writes fast hitting all the letters like little white rings standing up He let me hit some letters to make my own name. When he is hitting very fast we watch him threw the window sitting in the tree. Some times we thro acorns on his head then he gets up and chases us out of the tree.

The court room is where the prisoners get tried and sentenced to some weeks in jail. Pop always sits on the Bench why Bench It is not a bench at all. Benches are all in bottom of court. On the Bench Pop sits in a twiddling chair It has one leg with 3 feet and the seat goes round and round. If it goes round long enough the seat falls off at the top. One day we were playing on it and forgot to make it go down again. Next morning when Pop sat on it to try cases he waggled it too much and he fell off with the seat. All in court looked at him with surpris. He knew it was us. When we came back from school we got the punishing Once we went to sit in the very back bench with the people sit. We sat very still, but when Pop came on the Bench he saw us and said Chief constabel reemove those children and Piet came and

He knew it was us.

said in a soft voice Kom nou die bass wil juli nie hier he nie. So we had to go. Fathers and mothers can be very cruel not understanding about when they were small.

We would like to go up and see the poppom. But Pop says if you ever do that you know what to get. No one can get in becos the door is always locked. We sit at back of Mr. Lees litle hut and watch them come out of the tower. Mr. Lee is a round little man he is a town clerk. He lives next to us oposit to Crosses Hall and has a garden with peach trees. There is a wall between. walls are easy to climb no one sees us near the wagon house where the peach trees are close to the wall. we throw all the pips on the roof. Mr. Lees is mrs. simms father and Trixie lees who is going to marry with Alfred Main who has a brother Roland who thinks a lot of himself. Round the church is a square and a fence. There are few houses past the school only the jail and Miss Jollys house. There is a great hall crosses hall near us and Walkers house. It has a big space, here we play the soccer game. The

25

windows look like church windows. Sometimes one is open and we climb in to look. It is a funny kind of hall with fat pillars in the middle holding up the roof. Two upstairs ways Upstairs is another hall with funny little rooms round one end. Billie says the free Masons use them. Free masons are a secret society of only men. A new free mason has a terribel test to go in. He has to lie in a cofin with a rope round his neck and a sharp sword over his hed in one of the little rooms Billie says. A goat comes with great horns and pokes him. Why a goat. He has to know the whole Bible backwards and forwards. No girls can be free masoneses. Once a girl crept in a clock and listened to F.Ms having their secret sociaty and she was caught. They wanted to kill her but that would be a crime and F.Ms dont do crimes only good deeds so they had to make her a Fm and she was the only one. Now they very careful when they have secret sociaty and a man stands at door and does sentry go like the militery with a great sword in his hand. Other children told me all this. The men wear little aprons with rubies on them. Pop was a F.M. in Cradock. When I told him all about it he said what a lot of nonsense. dont you try any of that hiding in clocks. I would not hesitait to cut your head of if I found you. I said I never wish to belong to a secret society becos of too much talking. and Charles will never be a F.M. if he has to learn all that Bible he cant even rember one verse of Guy Fox Guy when we take the stufed guy round.

In Crosses hall now dances and bazars are held. In the upstairs hall they put tables for the dancing peopel to eat the food. Behind Midgleys hotel is a little shop. Mr. Smiths brother keeps it. He has lots of children who go to our church. He is one who takes the plate around. Last Sunday was Coots first time going to church and sat by Pop. When the plate came she put her hand in and tried to take all the money and howled when Mom shook her hand and had to be taken out. Mr. S. has Anna and Martha and Vera and Hazel and Tim and some others. Hazel is in my class. We both have to look after children in the afternoon. I must look after Coot and she look after Maddie. It is a great nuisens to us. They wont walk fast and then we have to carry them. They are fat and heavy to carry. Hazel goes in the shop behind the counter and gets sweets out of a bottle. A new kind of sweet round like a shilling with writing on it Sweetheart I love you, and be mine and give me a kiss. Silly words. I wish Pop had picked to work in a store than in any office. Magistrats never have money and only give children a penny on Saturday to buy sweets.

I found a librery, it is the most wonderfullest thing I have yet found heaps of books in a small room near Mr. Lees hut. The key is always on the window ledge anyone takes it and goes in. But no one only me and old Mr. Goldi ever goes there. There are heaps of books and magasins all lying mixed up together. There is an exercise book. You write your name and the books when you take them out. Old Mr. Goldi is a very kind man.

He cant climb up in the shelves to get the ones he wants. So I
get them for him. He tells me what to read and we talk about
them. and I write his in the book for him and he pats me on head
and gives me a tickey. When I am not looking at Coot I go
there to read. I have read all about a man called Sherlok Holmes
in Strand magazin. And Waverley novels and Lambs tales and
some others about Ladys and dukes. At night Pop likes saying
poetry he says pieces out of Biron and Shelley and Oliver Gold-
smith and tenyson. He remeber even better than me. He likes best
to say about Come one come all this rock shall fly its firm base
as soon as I, and about Macduff, and about the battle of Waterloo

Mr. Goldi.

did you hear it. no it was but the wind or the cart on the stony
street.

When it is dark we go over to sit in the water furrow with no
water in front of Sparkses house and some of the Lamonts and
Thelma come too and Miss Rena tells us stories. She tells stories
better than anyone else. She has thick golden hair. Gas is her
father. She has lots of peopel. Sonny on the bank and Hilda and
Ruby and Jeanie and Queenie and Bertie and Effie and Harry.
Mr. Sparks has a shop. Also Mr. Walker. Both shops are fast to
the houses. That must be fun. Mr. Walker has many. Gertie
and Jessie and Max and Albert and Thelma and Les and Ray.
Mr. Willie who keeps the shop with him is a bacheldor.

The day before Christmas Mr. Hill does this sort of thing. He throws in the street all sorts of things out of his shop for peopel to scrambel for. We wanted to scrambel too. But Mom just pushed us into Mrs. Bobs hotel and said Never it is only for poor peopel and natives. So we stood on the balconi to watch. I wished I was indeed a kafer that day. Charles got away at last and scrambled. He got a pair of shoes and Pop made him give them to our boy. The noise and shouting in the street was awful and the carts couldn't get thro the square. All the big girls of Sunday school went to decorat the church and the big boys went to the river to get the branches and leaves for it. Miss Jolly does the pulpit, only she must do that. we all do the seats and the sides. On the alter vases are special white flowers. The choir sings special songs and all wear the new dresses that day Mrs. Simms had a mouve one which made a crackling noise and a big purpel hat with a feather. Florence and I had new white muslin with daisies round our hats. Charles had a suit which scrached him. He hates scraching clothes. Coot went to Church but when plate time came she had to sit down. Charles says some boys at the back dont put their tickeys in the plate just pretent to and keep them. Thats cheating God.

Dr. Jock and Mrs. go once every month in the cart and horse to visit sick peopel in the country. He is a district serjen and has to do it. He is short and very funny. Dr. Hood is young and long and very solem. The dutch parson is Mr. Dominy. He is huge and has a short beard round his chin and we are afraid of him. He is the kind that doesnt know about children. He says let me look at your hands then he says now I know who helps mother. The ones who have the hard corns inside their hands help the mothers. When Pop told Mom she said hard corns indeed, their hard corns are becos of their helping themselves to so much troubel, anyone can see he is never had a family.

A farmer called Mr. Engelbrech brought Pop four guinea fowls alive. We put them in a hok. In the night they got out. We found 2 but not the other 2. All day we could hear them making their calling noise. Then Charles found they had fallen down the closet pit. A huge hole it is. Piet had to hook them out with a fishing rod. They were alright after they were bathed. Now we have to put planks on the seat when we finish.

When the Bishop comes a big boy is to get confirmation. He is Mark Raine. He is very clever and asking Mr. Damp so many things about God that Mr. Damp gets savige. Pop is now the chief warder man in Church taking the plate round to ask for money. On Sunday all must go. Some in morning some at nite putting on of best clothes and hats. In Church men take off hats women keep on hats. Pop puts on his tail coat and best black bouler hat. On other days he wears his old bouler hat. The other nite the lamp hanging over the front seat was going up high and making smoke. Mr. Damp was preeching a long sermon in the pullpit, and made signs to Pop to put it out and Pop must go and stand on High bak of seats and shaking backwards and side-wards becos tops are thin to stand on and coat tails flying and he not being able to reach lamp and nearly falling over backwards and much laughing was going on we laughed much too. and then Pop got his savige look and got slowly down and came and sat in his place and Mom was red in the face and just left the lamp with long smoke coming out and Pop said let the dam thing burn I not braking my neck for it, and then the dam thing went out which was lucky for all.

SCHOOL

This is the first time at this new school. I am in standard 4. The new sums of practise and fractions I cannot do. Why must children have it so hard to learn this strange thing about 20 doz. boxes at 2/6 each and 60 gross at shilling and a half and the mentle makes me giddy in my head to add so fast. Also a strang thing they learn here a new kind of singing called tonic Sulfur. It is a doh rey me fah singing. Teacher stands in front of a paper hang-

Mom said sit still hold fast child.

ing on the wall and points with a stick to the doh ray me writings up and down and evryone sings loudly to make a song. No piano it does not make sense to me. Why not singing like Pop and Mom. We sing nice things together Pop and Mom sing come where my

29

love lies dreaming and we all sing soldiers of the king my lad together without dohray me. Never will I get this right. The things I like best are essay and reading and poems. Charles says he doesnt like to do anything best. Today we having a holiday becos of a kind deed of a cat which went to die under the floor of the school. For many days the terribul smell of stink was in class. At last it could not be born any more. So everyone went outside and big boys chopped a hole in floor and took a light to see what it was. It was a big fat cat. much blown up. They had to put lime in and we played lovely games of rounders to let the stink out. Then we came home. Charles says it was a wild cat. Pop has again a horse and cart. This is a spider cart. Why spider. Mom is a good driver of horses. In East London when she was driving

It was terrible singing.

dog cart and a new horse Cecil bought and me sitting in seat with fat girl Truin and all going to fetch Pop at office. Then the new horse bolted running fast down the street and Mom said Sit still and hold fast the child and she pulling on the rains and at last the new horse stopped at office and Pop came out being savige only becos he thought we could be dead and said it was the ticks made him to bolt. Ticks I have not seen. Many ticks were eating on the new horse under his tail causing much pain to make him bolt. When ticks do that you rub fat on and they die.

Last week the singing inspecter came. His name is Raymond. He wears huge knikerbockers and thick stockings like a hunting man. He has a round red face and eyes like blue gooseberrys and golden curls on his head. He is indeed the most hatefullest man I know. This is what he did to us. He called everyone to come in the big room except the little ones and the big boys like Jack Long and Paulus who only do exams and no singing. Then we had to

do the doh ray me fah and tata te te things. Then the singing
He called out Benny and Charles first. They must stand in front
and he said now you two the long and the short you will sing for
us. But they didnt know one single song. Mr. R. was pointing
with a stick on the modelater. Not even the Blue bells of scotland
or minstrel Boy. He got angry and said in a roaring voice what
can you sing. sing anything and Charles said in a weak kind of
voice we can sing pretty Polly. Then sing it mr. R. shouted and
looked just like the picture of the Bull of bashan. And they began
to sing. It was terribel singing. Charles sang Pretty Polly pretty
poly whats whats oclock whats oclock in a low sort of voice and
Benny who is very long sang pretty poly pretty poly in a high kind
of squeaking voice becos of being afraid and all wanted to laugh
but being too frightend and then in the middle of the verse they
both stopped just as if they no more breath and Mr. R. shouted
waste of time waste of time two voiceles idiots in a singing class.
Send them out. Then he called Jessie and she sang on the modelater a nice song and then he called Gladys Armstrong and me. I
was trying to hide away but it was no help he saw me. I was
terified. Not a sound would come out of my mouth. Gladys was
shaking so I could feel her and he said what have we here the deaf
and the dum wheres your voice girl. I wanted to say you are just
a hateful bullie but no words came becos my heart was hitting and
jumping in my throat and strange noises in my ears. Then called
winnie and Gladys Long and said help the paralised mutes. That
night I had the night mare and dreamt Mr. R. was biting my head
off with his great white teeth. Pop had to sit with me a long time.
I told him about Mr. R. and he wrote to say I was never more to
do Doh ray me. Now I sit with the big boys who do exams and
with Charles and Benny when the singing lesson goes on and
learn to do sums. I hope some day this Bull of basham will be
punished for all he does to little girls and boys.

EDWARD 7

The new king is going to be crowned. Everyone is decorating
the house with flags and branches and chinese lanterns. There will
be a prize for the best house. Mr. Goldies is going to be fine
having 100 of little baby lanterns hanging all over. We have
bought lots of fat Chinese lanterns. Everyone is walking around
from the time it is dark to see the house lit up. Mr. Hills house
had big picturs of the new King and Qween in the windows with
lamps behind. They looked like real. They also had crowns
and thistels and other shapes all lit up. All houses had big and
little flags. But the green and blue c. lanterns were the best.
Sometimes they catch fire. In our windows we had flags lit up

and made God bless our king in little lamps. It was hard to do and much rowing went on everywhere. Mr. Gas Sparks was doing his door and we were doing our door and shouting at each other over the street and hoping ours would be better and Bertie fell off the ladder and pulled down all Mrs. Gases branches and Mr. Gas got in a rage and pushed his head in the branches and Charles was laughing and Mom bumped on the ladder and he fell down too and dint laugh any more. Miss Queenie and Miss Maggie and Miss Flora and all the ladies and peopel who have bicycles do a bicycle ride except Mr. Damp. They tied lighted lanterns on their bicycles and rode up and down the street pinging on their bells and singing. The next day we were going to have a big sports and picnic. But a telegram came to Pop to say the King was dying and could not be crowned he having caught a new kind of sickness no one knew before like a pen in sight is. He had to have his inside taken out with a sharp knife. Everyone felt awful. Mr. Gold and Mr. Hill got the prizes for the houses.

The King has got well again but no sports yet. We have had a photo taken. A man came and sat us on a bench in a row under the peper tree except Charles who had to stand behind Coot. We all dressed in our best sailor clothes and tied our hair with ribbons. The man said when I count 3 look all in this Box. When he said 3 Charles quickly pulled Coots hair and she opened her mouth very wide. The photo had to be done all over again. It is for Pop's sister who is in England becos she thinks we are black. Mom was very savige about black and Pop said if they had listened long ago to his godfather Bartle freer who brought me to this coutnry to fight the Zulus they would know better becos Governors dont let their godchild marry with Kafers.

The Dutch parson has the best house. It is a doubel story. It has a long garden at the back right to the river. In front on the side is a tennis and a croket court. His sister teaches music so does Miss Kate. I learn with Miss K. in the scotch Church room. In the street are lots of houses going to the river. I wish we had one. Mrs. Simms and old Mr. Vice have one with the nicest garden much orange trees. Here there is a path in the garden where we go down to swim in the river. Only girls becos it is not deep. After school we all go to swim. We must not touch the fruit. Sometimes we pick up that lies on the ground. On the square Mr. Billy Band a small man with a very big wife keeps the bank. Dr. Hood lives near the bridge. His wife is very thin and rides on a horse very well. Mr. Hill has a man who keeps the books he is Wilson. I go with Margie and Evie to visit Mrs. Wilson on Saturdays. We call her Aunt Mabel. She lives in our street and has a garden with big stoep and many oak trees. She gives us ginger beer and cakes and has many toys and books. I always have the books. She has no children and never gets cross. I like going there more than any place.

Mr. Damp gave a concert for Church money. In the court house.

32

It was only the second concert I have seen. The other was in Maraisburg when the militery gave one. It was cristy Minstrel one and Mr. Johnny Oosthuizen and Pop were the end men in the row of singing peopel. They had to dress like coons and black faces and make jokes and call each other Moses. Mr. Johnny made his head to go open at the top when he laughed so it looked as if his brains were there. They sang nice songs like Shine shine moon while I walk with Dina dear and down on the swanee river. Afterwards Bartelman my friend sang Tommy Atkins and his friend sang our loger is such a nice young man and Mom said it was a rude song and we not to sing it. No rude or even nice songs were sung at Mr. Damps concert. They played long things 2 peopel at one piano. A man blew on a flute. Mr. Sid Sparks sang and they sang Alice Benbolt and Tom Bowling and Mrs. Clem sang a funny song a cup of camminile tea and another lady sang a very strange song the watermelon growing on the Wine. Mr. Damp said a long dull poem. It seemed as if it was going on forever and Mark Raine was the one to be pulling up and letting the curtain down. He was standing behind Mr. Damp and pretending to be winding him up with a handle and we were laughing and it was not a laughing poetry. Charles and I laughed the loudest till we saw Mr. Sid Sparks coming to chase the boys at the back. The lady who sang about a watermelon made strange kind of face and rolled her eyes to all. When it was over lots of peopel came to eat food at our house. Charles and I found a jug of cream. We had never tasted it befor I drank it all like milk but much nicer. But having a weak stumick I got the bilios attack in the night. Pop was holding me over the bucket and was saying this is the last concert that old sky pilot gets me into. Why sky pilot. The next day at supper Mom said Cecil I think Florence is getting the Vituses dance. Look at the awful faces she is pulling. Charles said No it is only the watermelon growing on the wine. no one can do it properly.

THE GAS LIGHT

A great thing is going to happen in this place. Mr. Bob is putting a new kind of light in his hotel called GAS. Every room will have it. We all went to see it being lighted for the first time. Becos of the gas Mr. and Mrs. Bob gave a party. The gas is wonderful. In every room is a lamp fast to the wall. Some like footballs hang in the middel of the roof. Some have little vases round the light yellow and pink and white. Inside the vase is a thing that looks like chalf. You turn a little tap on the pipe and put a match on the chalk and it makes a noise like a ginger beer popping softly then there comes a nice bright yellow light. Outside the hotel at the corner is a light. It was a great glass ball. To make the light shine Mr. Jack had to climb on a high ladder to light. An awful thing happened. when he put the match in the light blew up just like the pompom gun shooting and knocked Mr. Jack down and far away. But he didnt break his neck or anything and the man who made the gas ran quickly and turned the tap off and said it was a LEAK. I would be mended next day. Then we all went in the sitting room and Mr. Jack went to the Bar and every one had a lovely party drinking strong drinks and we drank lemenade. It looks like fairy lights to see the Bobs hotel with all the gas in it now. The gas is made in a machine in the yard and has a strange stink like rotting eggs. The light does not stink like that. Pop says all big towns have this kind of light. Here we have only six parafen lamps on a pole at the corners. We always walk in the dark. Peopel who drive in the night take a lantern. When it is full moon in the street we all play I spy kick the tin at the market bell. At half past 8 we have to go home to do our homework and Bertie Sparks and Amy Waker always win. Mr. Gas Sparks has a brother Mr. Jim. He is also a law man. He has a very hooked nose and red beard. We went on a visit with him.

GRAHAMSTOWN

Pop had to go to Grahamstown with Mr. Jim for a case. He took me and charles with. We started in a cape Cart at 1 oclock in the night to drive to Cookhouse to get the train. Mr. Sparks had a basket of food and we had one too. At Cookhouse we drank hot coffee and ate food out of the baskets. The stars were bright all night. Pop and Mr. Jim told us names of many Big belt and little belt and the Cross. We came to Gt. in the evening. It is a big station with lots of noise. Men were running up and down it shouting outside the train windows Boots to hell boots to hell. Why could they be shouting these swear words. Pop said No they are shouting Woods Hotel Woods hotel. The man of Woods took our port man toes and we got out and climbed in a buzz and drove in the streets all lit up with the gas lights like fairy lights on strings. Here in Gt is a museum. We saw stuffed elephants and lions and bucks the first time. We went in the Botanics garden and saw a fairy dell made by another man called Woods. It is called Woods Grotto with ferns and rocks and little water falls. It was lovely. We went to see Mr. Gowie who has a garden for selling. We also went to see the man who sells the pointer dogs. He buys the pups from us. We had our photos taken at a proper place. Charles had to stand behind the chair and behave. He did not get the chance to pull on my hair. There is a cathedrel here. It does not look up to much. Not for a cathe-

34

dral. Not as nice as our dutch church. We saw a new kind of cheese at our hotel called gorge and zola. It has worms in it. Mr. Sparks and Pop et of it. I had to get up and go out becos of the smell and the worms jumping. Even when I am old I will never eat of chees like that. Charles says he cant either. We bought a canary in a cage to take to Florence. We take it in turns to look after. In the train and the cart it had to covered with a cloth or it would die of fear. It sings.

I think Mr. Damp is indeed a horrid man. When he saw our photo he said she looks like Alice in wonderland with her long neck and Charles looks like a chesire cat with its grin going away. I wished I belonged to Mr. Makles church. He only pats you on the head and says Lassie girl, never about how you are looking.

Pats you on head and calls you Lassie.

I found a pictur of the devil in a book in the libery. He has horns and a pointed tail like dragon flames coming out of his mouth and a long fork. Mr. Damp says God sees all you do. All your sins are written down in a big book for jugement day like stealing and glutony and swearing and lying. Florence says if you just take a few is that stealing. Becos of the peaches. I said God must be a very busy watching all in the whole world like how does He do it. I would never like to be Him. Mr. Damp says we all impossible. We told Coot about the devil and his fork and fire and how he poked you in it and about absalom hanging up by his hair on a tree and we showed her the picturs of the childs bible Pop bought us and she got a night mare . . . Why mare.

Dr. Room the school inspector has been. He has just got a wife Teacher said he hoped he would be kinder to all pupils now he has a wife. it isnt always so. He went to Germany to find her. He has a very long head and blue eyes with big glasses. He looks very fierce but he is better than Mr. Raymond but not very much. He snaps. You can see he does not know about children yet. Charles failed. He always fails and must be put up. Gladys armstrong was so afraid she cried. Mr. R. said in a nasty voice how pathe tick. perhaps his wife will make him know that little girls cry of fear. We all passed. I was so glad I tied Glads Long and Gladys Arms long plaits together where they are hanging down in front of my desk. When they stood up their heads jerked together and Miss Lily gave me 50 lines to learn. I know heaps of poems so it did not matter. I said the sky lark. We go to a new teacher now Mr. Hanekom. He is savige.

END OF WAR

The war is ended. Pop says now the militry will leave him alone. The Pompom has gone off the church and sandbags it was a shame to put it on a church. At last we could go up, without telling. Some of the steps are broken it was not easy. we had to jump. When we came home Mom found out and rowed us. She said you could break your necks there Mr. Damp is going away for a long time. He gave Florence a book called Struel peter. A strange kind of book. He does not like me becos of my asking too much. I dont think much of struel silly rymes about silly looking peopel like I dont want any soup today or take the nasty soup away and getting thinner a fat boy. no one says that about food. This week we went to place in the countrey in a cart it is called Krommee. It is a hotel belonging to 3 ladies called Weelden. Pop went to buy erfs to build his own house on. We staid all day becosc Pop said they were hard nuts to crack. why nuts. There father was dead. In the yard of this K. hotel is a long house made of glass in its sides. It is full of ferns. In middle is a walk where you stand to look. They grow all over and are beutiful. Six times I went in to look. It was like Woods grotto. I wish we could have a fern house like this. The men who live near are called farmers and Nilands. Pop got 3 erfs near the jail. We are going to build a house soon. It will be near the school and Miss Jolly. We go every afternoon with pop to visit in the jail. That is his work. Mr. Jailer salutes and gets out the keys on a long thin chain like silver and we walk round the cells. The prisoners jump up and Pop says any complaints and then they get locked in again and we go to kitchen to look the food they eat. Prisoners have to sleep on hard plank beds. They roll up there blankets. Some times we talk to Mrs. Jailer. We tell her about Cradock where we saw a galloes for hanging men. 3 Kafers were being hanged on this galloes becos they did an awful murduring. They caught a poor farmer becos they did not like him and tied him fast on the railway line and the train cut him in bits. Pop had to go out with police to arrest them and see the poor farmer. Then the juge came and tried them and he put the black cap over his head and said they must be hanged by the neck until they dead. A man came from Capetown to be the hangman. He made a steeple thing. We went with Pop in the jail and saw it. They tried it with a heavy sack of sand to see if it works for hanging. The hangman took charles on it and said now you can say you have stood on a galloes. But not me. Pop was there for the hanging. The Kafers all said they did it. They could eat anything they like

He was savige using swear words.

before they hanging. They ate grilled chops. Pop said the hangman quickly took a cigeret out after the hanging and smoked it becos his hand was shaking.

After Pop comes out of the jail we go for a walk to take the

37

pointer dogs and train the carier pigeons we carry them in little basket and let them out to fly home. Pops pigeons are very good coming from East Londen in a few seconds. We like best to go to Mr. Alecs drift. Here is an old Mill House. It has a garden with thick quince hedge round it. They the geel vleis kind. We all wanted one to eat. Pop got me one and for Charles then Florence wanted one, not wanting to bite out of ours. Then when Pop was getting one his bouler hat fell inside the thick fence. Then he swore and laid down on his stumick to try and hook it with his blackthorn stick and then his stick went in and he could not get it, and he was savige using swear words and becos he had to knock at door and ask lady inside and tell what he had done and pay for quinces. Then the lady gave us more quinces and Pop and she talked a long time about England and honesty is best policy and Charles said with us it is not always so.

A new man teacher has come to teach. We call him BROEKS becos he wears such wide trowsers. He never shouts at you. Only throws chalk and hits every time. He is a good teacher, at last he is making me to understand my sums and my dutch spelling.

We had a Sunday school picnic. First we had our prizes the week before. I got a Bible. I would have like Knights of Round Tabel or Gulivers travels. Miss Jolly gave me a lovely plant in a pot becos I had got so well with my salms. It was called Chinese balsam and we keep it in the dining room windows. Mom said at last one was getting good out of church. Charles got disgrace. He only had 8 tracks for the whole year. I gave him two of mine and he gave me a small glassie for it (marble). Mr. Damp knew he had only got 6 tracks he said where did you get others. He said I swopped for them. There was a good row about swop. We went on a wagon to picnic. Far past Mr. Alec's farm on a nice flat grass place with trees. The teachers and all little children and food baskets went on the wagon. In the afternoon all fathers and mothers came in carts and we had sports. In the race Mabel Long fell and broke her arm and had to go home with Dr. Jock. He mended it with planks she said it was agony. She carries it in sling and cant do any home work. Some are wishing to have the broken arm and not do any homework too. When we came home from the picnic we played a game Jolly miller, becos we had to walk and if you play this game you dont see how long the way is becos you are running to catch the peopel in front all the time. We sang wait for the wagon.

It is now Hopskotch time. Mom says it is a curse becos of wearing out of shoes. Florence is the worst child with shoes. She must have the boots with iron protectors on bottom. The bootmaker puts them on with hammer. They can make you slip but Florence does not care she is always kicking stones and is a rough child. Simon Donald has gone away. A new one Jack came he has also gone and Willie Marais is now in Pop's office. He is a good looking person. He runs the fastest at races and wears a blue silk shirt and short running trowsers. We also had Miss Lily to teach us for a term. She reads out of Alice in Wonderland and told us a funereal cost lots of money 300 pounds. Pop said dont any of you die now if it costing so much, becos you will all be buried in the pawpers grave. I shall be bankrupt.

Today a Temperince lady came to school. Her name is Henrietta like mine. Not a nice name. Why must chuldren be called after grandmother. Mine wont ever be. All schoolchildren had to come in big room to listen to this lady talking about strong drink. She said it is the food of Satan. She put 2 picturs on the blackboard. One was a great fat red heart and one was a small pink heart. The fat heart was the brandy drinkers and the pink

Temperence Lady.

heart the water drinkers. The lady said Now all look at these hearts and then you can tell me what heart you would like to have. And Lindsay who was in one stood up and said I would like to have that nice fat heart and teacher put him down and Frances stood up and said I want the nice pink small hart and everyone was releaved. and all talked about it at lunch time. We think Miss Henri should go and hang those picturs in the Bar, becos many peopel go there and must have the fatharts. We told Pop at supper and asked him why not and he said Good Lord what next will you think of and I said why not Miss Henri says those drinking peopel have the fat hearts. And he said be quiet you will know when you get big. It is too much to tell now. That is what big peopel always say to children. When you get big you forget all about the things when you were small. Now we belong to a sociaty and wear a little blue ribbon. I put mine in my butterscotch tin. But Charles got his stuck in the bird lime we were making and it got ruened. We are going to catch birds. I don't care much for catching birds. We tried in the garden with a seeve on a stick which you pull with a string hiding away in a tree. But I always feel so sorry. When no one is looking I let them out again.

39

SCHOOL GUY, FOX AND LANCERS

Mr. Johnny Bok who is the chief teacher here has gone away to
be an Inspector at a place Kronstad. Two new teachers have
come. They are Mr. Gerrie he is an Englishman and Mr. Patrick
he is an Irishman. Mr. Gerrie is thin and looks very sick Mr. Pat
is fat and rosy and looks very well. He is sometimes jolly and
says begora. He is coming 2 nights in the week to teach Charles
extra lessons becos he never passes when Inspectors come. He
teaches me analysis about all those clauses now I know. Pop says
it is a great cost for him but must be done. This month is to be
Guy Fox. We are making in our street our own G. Fox all our
friends helping. The big men make a great G. Fox with 1000
crackers in its stumick. They put a mambakkie on its face. We

Mr. Gerrie and Mr. Patrick.

all buy the cheap mambakies in the shop to wear for walking the
Guy. We make only a little one with pajamas. Mom helped us
to stuff it with papers and rags and put a few crackers in it. The
boys made a seat to carry it on. Charles had to be the one that
says the ryme about rember fifth of November the gunpowder
treson plot and never be this day forgot. For a whole week he
learnt it every night. But when we went on the night he only got
as far as forgot and then he also forgot all the rest and Alec had
to say it. We got tickeys and pennies from the peopel. Then we
came back and burnt the guy in the yard and bought ginger beer
at Mr. Gases shop with the money. It was fun. Then we waited
late for the big men to come. We could hear them shouting far
away. When they came it was very fearful. They looked like
brigans Pop said and the Guy was a great huge one and fearful
too. The men stamped and made a great row and said a long

40

poem and shot a cracker and Pop gave a shilling. When you dont give money they throw rocks on roof and shout SHABBY shabby Pop says they dont buy ginger beer with there money they buying something warmer. There is a young lady come to stay with Mrs. Wilson. She has a very nice voice for singing. Her name is Maud. She is having a concert for the Church in the crosses hall. Charles and I have to be in this concert and Violet Vice. Violet is saying a poem about curfew shall not wring tonite. There will be lots of other singing 2 peopel are singing a thing called a duet a screeching sort of song about o that we two are maying. When they finished many claped loudly and said encor. We had to act in a thing called sharad. Charles is in awful rage about this sharad. He had to be the dunce and stand in a corner on a stool with dunce cap on his head. Pop said why you in a fury you must be quite used to it after all these years. and Charles told me it is nothing to be a dunce in school where Benny and Tim are also dunces but who likes to be dunce in front of all people in Adelaide coming to look at you all other boys will laugh at me. It was no use to talk or even howl. Fathers and mothers dont know about those things any more. After the concert there was a dance. Mom staid to watch it and we staid too. Pop did not come to concert. He was at home to look after Coot and Florence. He said he was glad he not having to listen to all that. We liked to watch the dance. It is the first time we have seen the dance. What a funny thing it is. We thought Mr. Sid and Miss Alice were the best in the dance. Mr. Sid wore nicest shiny slippers called pumps why pumps and pointed his toe the best of all the men dancers in a thing called a padda kar. Mrs. Simms only danced in the wals. She is the most statly Mom says. Trixie Lee laughs a lot when she dancing as if great fun. The wals is a strange thing. The men hold the ladies round the middle and turn very fast one way then they turn very fast the other way. This is called reversing. It makes us giddy to watch this thing. Those who cant do the turning just push the lady down the room backwards. I wonder how she never hits the pillars that hold the roof up. It is a dangeros way of having fun this dancing. The most dangeros is the LANCERS why lancers. Lancers are horse soldiers. The lancers made a lot of noise stamping and clapping their hands and shouting ladies in the center. They ran in and out holding hands and bowing to each other with one hand on the stumick and some of the ladys were swung high and nearly fell down. When they finished the men wiping the sweat off their faces. We went home after the lancers. It is just across the road not far to walk Pop was savige becos we so late. He said what an hour to be staying out at night. We said we saw lancers. I said, Pop why do they call them lancers he said being very savige. becos they prancing like cavelry horse and screeching like hoeligans no civilised man will make such an idiot of himself. Mom said that just becos you cant do them I am going again next month becos Mrs. Simms and

I have to be lady Pat for the dance and I am shaperoening Miss Maud and Miss minnie. Why Lady Pat. I must ask when Pop not in rage. Pop said Dam the Lady pat and then we all went to bed.

This has not been a good week at school. Charles and I both got punishings and it was not fair. All becos of doing that honesty is the best policy . . . I always have to help Charles with his homework or he would be getting a caning every day at school. I do it badly then no one will know. He had to do essay on George Washington. The teacher reads the story in school 3 times and gives you the hard words to copy down. Then you must come home and write it in your exercise book. But Charles did not rember what the story about G. Wash was about becos he was not listening trying to make his christmas bees go back in the match box. So I guessed and told him what to write. He wrote "G. Wash greatest words were I cant tell lie father I choped down your cherry tree and his father must have been a different kind of father to ours becos he praised George up but if I choped down the tree in our back yard my father would get out his strap when I told him I cant tell a lie I choped down your tree. This shows that honesty is not always the best policy becos it depends on your fathers and mothers." Charles said it was a very good essay. But when we came to school the story about G. Wash was not a bit like that and Mr. Pat said who helped you to write this and Charles would not say But mr. Pat guessed and said Iris did you help to write this and I was like G. Wash I said yes I did. Charles got caned and I got kept in becos Mr. Pat said we were trying to be smart. Charles says it just shows all peopel are not like G. Washes father. When you tell the truth in Adelaide all you get is not praising but a caning which shows that honesty is not the best policy. It is a lie. Charles says from now when it suits he will tell lies becos anyway you mite not get found out, and anyway if you are found out or tell truth you get caned anyway. It is all too much for me. I have not decide yet what policy I must do. Mom told me a Lady pat was a lady who was married and had to go to dances to look after all that are not married. What a lot of rot is that.

POOR SCHOOL AND THE RIVER AND DRIFT AND EELS

Here is another school called the Poor school. Miss Kate Mary's aunt keeps it. Her father is a scotch parson she has a sister Miss Grace. Yesterday Lily fought a fight with Steve. We made a ring round. She has red hair. She can fight but she scratched too. Charles said that was cheating. Girls always cheat. it is not true. She fought becos they teased her little sister. A big boy came and stopped u\. It made her nose bleed. I held her books.

At break times the girls play a game called French and English. You pick sides with a captin for each. Gladys Long and Winnie

Davis run fastest and are always captins. You draw a long line in the street and one side stands on one side of line and one side on other side face to face. Each one must first bring a stone and put it in a nest far behind your own line. Then you jump up and down on your side of line and try and get past a girl and fetch a stone out of the other nest. If you get caught you are a prisoner and have to stay in the nest. It is a fine game with many to play. We also play a lot of skipping and rounders and hop scotch, which wers shoes out awfully Many time we take off shoes and play with bare feet, which is easy for picking up the goen with your toes. The boys play marbles and tops and catapults and catching birds and shooting with daisy guns. They carry their marbles in bags some have 100s big glassies and small glassies blood alleys and commons. You shoot the marbles out of the ring with a big glassy. A blood alley is the most precous of all marbles becos of having red spots in it. Tops are exciting. Sometimes they end in fight. Some boys have four tops one for kipping. They throw into a ring and try and kip other boys top out with a spinner. They have a special kind of string. Some put wax on I just spit on mine. Tim can make his sing and so can Stevie. They play cricket and soccer. Sometimes they let girls play too. I always keep the goal. You have great troubel with the bladder it is often bursting and cost a lot of money to buy.

There is a location at the top of the town where the Kafers live and a Block by the river where the Tots live. Above the Block is the old Mill and over the drift on the other side is a farm of a nice old bacheldor man Mr. Alec Pringle. You cross big stepping stones to come to this farm. We were visiting with Mr. Alec one day and Pop was helping Florence over step stones and Mr. Alec was talking much saying observe mr. Vaughan observe and Pop let Florence fall in. He said it was becos of having such a bad stumick ache and being in a dreadful hurry to get home quickly.

The nicest picnic we have are at this drift the willos are very big so big you can swing right over the water. The water is very deep here. Vinks nests hang all over the river. They look like little baskets and make a chatering noise. Miss Calagans and men who work in the bank took us all on river in the boat. The first time we ever been in a boat. We had to sit very still It was wonderful. They row with 2 long poles called ors oars we went down to another weer. where you get a farm called Haddon. It used to be Hollands now it is van der Merwes. A weer is a stone wall built across the river. It makes the water very deep and strong. We had to turn back becos it would be dangeros to go near the weer. We went all the way under the red bridge right to Mr. Alecs farm We passed the mouth of the Kowie r. On the banks if you go quietly you can see the platans and lakavans and sometimes great awful crabs in holes in bank . . . The willow branches hang far in the river. Under them the boat went for us to have tea. But the water is deep and muddy and makes me fraid. There are eels in

43

the river. When it floods the boys go to fish for them. I dont like eating eels. When I saw the first Charles brought it looked like a snake. it made me want to throw up. Pop and the others eat it for brekfast. Florence said it tasted like mud. Pop told us when he was in australia he eat snakes. The aboridgness catch them with hooked stick while they are wriggling they quickly chop of heads and poison cant go down. They cook them in pot over coals. They look just like eel and taste like chiken. He only eat it once when he went with Lord Goch to chase some aborigness who murdured a white man and eat him. They dont do that there now. I am glad our black man dont do that here not even in Riebecks time did they eat off white peopel. In my own mind I beleive eels are just water snakes. Who can tell only God. Never shall I eat off eel.

THE CHRISTIAN SOCIETY AND THE CIRCUS

Another lady has come to teach us. Lady teachers do not stay long in this school. Her name is Miss Cora. She is like a small sparrow and has a velvit bow in her hair which is a grey color She is old and very thin and much timid. She is also a very holy lady. Holy people are not laughing a lot. Why. The other day a boy laughed in church becos he was reading I must not marry with my grandmother in the pray book and Mr. Damp rowed him in front of all. Sometimes it is hard to know Only bad peopel are fun. Miss Cora is not fun. She teaches us French a hard languige with a funny way of saying everything to sound like ong. She is having a christian sociaty for us. It is only for girls. We stay after school and pray. I didnt want to stay but Mary was begging me. Miss Cora read out of Bible and then we all knelt down beside our desks and then she said Now mary will offer up a prayer and Mary made a real lovely pray. I was thinking how lovely it was then Miss Cora said Iris will now offer a prayer. and all I could think of was Gentle Jesus meek and mild and the Grace Pop says when he remebers to say about for what we are about to receive make us truly thankful. And then the sweat began to run down my stumick like it always does when I get fright and all were waiting for me to pray and befor I knew what I was saying I said twinkle twinkle little star, and I am not going to Christian sociaty any more it is too woriyng to pray loudly. It is only parsons can pray loudly.

A most exciting thing has come this week. It is a CIRCUS. Mr. pagels circus It is camping near the market bell. We are all going to it. Then the band went round in the street playing loudly and peopel came behind on elephants and funny clowns all painted up and beeutiful ladies on shining horses. When school

44

was out we all ran to watch near tent, a great high tent and the boys were lying on there stumicks trying to creep underneath and men with whips chasing them out. We sat in the high up seats which are cheaper than the low down seats. We are many and it would cost lots of money to sit in low down seats. I prefer high

Circus. It was too wonderful.

up becos of lions being so near to low down seats. It was too wonderful. The beeutiful ladies wore hardly any clothes and swang in the air on things called trapeasies and rode on galloping horse jumping through rings of fire and the clown did funny things and funny jokes and dressed in pajamas. Best of all was Mr. Pagel. He is young with golden hair and must be the strongest man after Samson and Golyth. He stood on a ladder and picked up a white horse with a broad band round its belly. He picked up with his teeth holding the band. The horse made strang grunting noises as if it was not pleasant to be held in the air by the belly. I was very glad when he was let down again. Mr. Pagels teeth were still alrite. He also lifts up big things called dumbells. Why dum. Lots of men tried to lift them with 2 hands and never moved them. Mr. P just takes one hand and lifs just like a stick up. We were all sad when the Circus went away. I saw the lovely ladies the next day. They were most awful looking in the day. I asked

Pop why and he said becos of the greese paint they putting on at night to make them lovely I think lots or hijeous peopel ought to know about this wonderful greese paint.

Now we are going to have a circus in our yard. Flor. will be Mr. Pagel becos she can shake her legs and arms best like he did when he picking up the horse. Her legs are fatter than mine. Bell the pointer will be the white horse. She is thin and not too heavy for teeth. Charles will be the boss and the clown and wear his pajamas. He said I could be the ladies who swing in trapeasies becos I am so thin. I can only swing from one branch in peper tree to other like an ape, and wear hardly any clothes. It is a pity we cant get the greese paint. We are letting all children come and pay one penny to look then we will get some money. But we were stopped having our circus becos Pop came when we were practising and saw us when I was swinging in the blue gum and Flor was lifting Bel up the ladder. There was a great rowing and he said What will they think of next. Break their b- necks and be a good riddens.

Another strange thing has come here. It is an Indian jugler. Such a wonderful thing it is. I have never seen befor. The world is full of strang things The Indian is the thinnest man I have ever seen dressed in a strange fashon. Very long thin bare legs with big toes and no shoes. On his head he had a great rolled up cloth and he had a little Indian child who carried his baskets of magic. He came to Pop's office and asked if he could make magic. Pop called lots of peopel. we all sat round in a ring not too near becos of the snakes. Then he took out his magic things like brass dishes and sticks and things and one basket no one must go near for it was snakes. Then he took a thing which looked like 2 sticks and blew on it. It made a kind of noise like Bartelman made on his bagpipes at MB when he was marching in front of Major Pens house when he ate his dinner. And when he blew all of a sudden the lid of the basket come open and great awful snake with flat head came out and crept in front of Indian and stood up on its tail and swung up and down like as if it was dancing. It did other things and then it went back in its basket and the Indian did other magic on cloths. He said Put leetel sant and sprinkled it and then we saw magic things to come and go. All gave him money. Now we are going to make the Indian gugler too. But Pop heard us when we were talking and said nothing of the sort putting leetel sant indeed putting poison it will be. So we did not do jugler. Concert people are coming here from Cookhouse to do Concerts, and always they giving Pop complementary tickets becos of lending the court house to do it. But Pop and Mom always give tickets to us and we now see many concerts.

Now it is hunting season. We take turns to go with Pop to shoot. We hold the pointer dogs on the strap. Bell is the best pointer never making a mistake like ponta always she pointing at birds. Bell has it hard her leg being bent where Ponta bit her

46

when she was pup. Now she always walks funny way like Mr. Ostrelyn in Cradock becos one of his big toes was chopped off.

In the gardens by the river are many orange trees. Mrs. de Beer has the best and always letting us come and pick after school. Miss Jones is a very jolly lady but she still rides on a bicycle. The post Office is in a house. Not like the smart one Mrs. Oost had in Mbg. It is near the Dutch Church. Near the post of. is Mr. Williams. he is a blacksmith with many children nearly all boys. Mr. Thomson is a wagon maker He is on the square near Bobs hotel. He has many children. The girl is Pearly Next to him is Mrs. S-. She is a widow lady and has

But she still rides a bicycle.

Miss Grace and Miss Flora. Mr. Damp lives with them. They have a lovely grape vine at there house. Mis Flora is the prettiest lady who isnt married yet. She has black hair and red cheeks.

We are having a holy time in the church It is called Lent. In lent is the time when all must fast. We must give up something we like to eat like sugar and sweets and cakes men must give up smoking. Pop has not given up anything it is not fair he is a warden man. On Good Friday is the holiest day of all. Then you must eat nothing all day and be quiet and not play. Only fish and hot cross Buns you may eat. We eat many buns Mr. Syd Sparks made them and put a cross on every one. All must go to Church. We all went to Church. Only Coot stayed behind with Ellen. It was a long church. when we came home Ellen said The vark has got out of its hok and is eating in Masters potatos. Then it was a great shouting and running to the garden and Pop with his coat

47

tails flying and his bouler hat tight on his head in front holding his blackthorn stick and saying catch him and Charles got him by the tail but pig squeeled loudly and ran and Pops said you fool catch him by leg tail is no good for holding pigs and we all ran Florence and Coot too only not Mom who was calling leave the pig you spoiling your good clothes but all ran and pig ran and Pop put his blackthorn between pigs legs and pig turned round and ran between Pops legs and Pop fell over and we all laughed and Mom said this is disgracing the Holy day and then Charles got pig by leg and we all got a leg and pulled pig back in hok. Pig squeeled loudly. Then we all went to wash and eat dinner of sardins and bun We talked about Judas I said I feel sorry for Judas beng such a wicked sinner Mr. Damp says we must be sorry for sinners and if Judas hadnt done that terribel deed would we have had a church Pop and Pop said enough that is enough we will not discuss Judas any more and we all went out to feed pig and see if he alright. When winter comes poor pig must become bacon and ham this is cruel I feel sorry for pigs. After Good Friday came Easter Day. It is a great day of rejoicing. We all went to church all must have nice new clothes and all must help decorat the Church day before with white flowers. When we came to steps of church Mr. Damp was standing there bending down to all and holding his hands like pray and looking very holy. We all went in fast becos Mom pushed us. Every one had nice new clothes Mrs. Simms had the nicest a big hat with a ostrich feather in it. They sang nice hymns the best one was allelua the fight is or the battle won. Much money was put in the plate like halfcrowns and not tickeys. Pop has to count the money afterwards. He said it was a good hawl.

FORT BEAUFORT

We have got a shift on. To Fort Beaufort. Pop went in his spider today. We are coming in a cart next week. A new magistrat called Mr. Hermans and his wife will live in our house here. We will be in a residensy in F.B. Mr. Nailhard is the magistrat who is going away to England for holidays.

We drove past the Krommehotel when we came to F.B. Fort B. is prettier than Adelaide, but it will never be nice to us. We came over a bridge. The river is Kat. Bridge is called Victoria. Here is a tall fat looking fort like an upside down Malays cap. It is called Martelo tower. The militery of long ago built the fort and the bridge when the kafers were dangerous to us. There are lots of barracks here where the soldiers lived long ago. Now only lunaticks live in them black lunaticks. Men loons live on one side of the town and lady loons live on the other. We live near the men. Here is a lovely park called a GROVE. Why grove. also a nice square better than adelaide and a nice town hall with a steple like a church. I wish all these things were not better than adelaides. There is a nice court house like at Maraisburg only this one has canons and a canon balls standing in front of it. That is wonderful. no one has yet told me how they shot off those canon balls long ago. now our canons have long shot. Bartelman showed me. They say load train FIRE. How did they carry those old round heavy balls about. Pop says the canons staid up on the fort. how did they get up there. on their backs.

Here are shops Whites shop and Wilsons shop and estments all on the square. Also a doubel storey hotel called comercial and a small librery with a lady to look after it. There are people with the same name as us, but not relating, becos we are Welsh Pop says but what an awful languige that is, he says. F.B. people think there town with a grove and a steple and a lonatick place is much better than Adelaide. We will never think so. I truly hate this place becos it is better than Adelaide.

We went to stay at the doubel storey hotel which Mr. Bobs brother John keeps. Its right name is Waterloo. Was it do with the battle Wellington fought in 1815. no one knows here. Mr. Nailhard came after supper to see Pop and Mom. Miss Merry his daughter came with becos they had to talk about the furni-chure, Mr. Nail was leaving us in the residensy. We were all sent

I said wake up this is my bed.

49

to bed. Florence and I had to sleep in óne room There were 2
beds. When I opened the door to put Florence to bed, a man
was sleeping in one bed, making very loud snores. I sailed down
the banisters and went to tell Mom about the man in the bed. Mom
was talking and Miss Mery was talking and all were talking and
would not listen to me about the man in bed. Pop said go to bed
at once I said must we sleep in that room with the snoring man,
and he said dont bother me any more you a most anoying child.
So I went and put Florence to bed and the man went on snoring
and I poked him and said wake up this is my bed. But he never
woke. So I sat with Florence and read my book and when nailards
had gone and Mom came to see if we asleep she gave a loud
screech when she saw the man. She said you never know when
this child is telling truth or making up. Then Pop and Mr. John
and the man who works in the Bar all came and threw the snoring
man out. He was DRUNK. I got clean sheets on my bed and
went to sleep.

We have moved in Residensy. This R. makes up for every thing
we dont like in F.b. It is a great stone house with a wonderful
garden of 20 erfs. Long ago it was a military horspital. It has
great rooms like court houses and many bedrooms and long ver-
andas at back and in front and great water tanks like huts and fruit
trees many and flowers and a great fern house but smaller than
the one at Kromme. We have our own piece of river to swim and
go and fish. It is too wonderful. But there is also a sunday school
here and the parson is a very holy man like Mr. Damp Already he
has been to tell Pop about us coming to Sunday school. Florence
has to go too. Now she will suffer. But she says she dont care.
She never cares. There is a man who is getting ready to make a
railway line. We are going to have a railway line from Cookhouse to F.B. Adelaide will also have a railway line. The mans
name is mr. Percy. He calls Mr. Nailhard old Tintacks Why tintacks. The parsons name is Rector. His S. school is worse than
Mr. Damps He asked me a thing I never heard befor. What is
your duty to your neibour. It is in a catecism I have never
heard of this catecism. He said now you will say your duty to
your neibor after me in front of all the sunday school. horrid man
all were listening to me saying this long duty about my duty is to
love him as myself. Which is a lie right away how can you do that
when you dont feel like it. I have made up my mind that this S.
School now is an awful worry. For it is Latin I must learn and
have a friend at the Sunday school She is Violet She goes to the
convent. We all go to the Public School. Mr. Hector is the prin-
ciple. I am in his class a very fierce man the fiercest I know
School now is an awful worry. For it is Latin I mus learn and
ι new thing called geometry. The Latin is not so bad, only the
naddest ways of saying O table, to or for a table, by with or
from a table in mensa mensas mensae mensam. But the euclid.
Pop says euclid was a very clever man who thought a lot and one

A very fierce man.

day he thought about geometry and cried out Eureka I have found it and then he wrote all his euclid books. I wish he had never found it, all these lines and a b c d e letters at the ends of them and then when you have finished it you say QED which dont make any sense to me. I shall suffer much becos of this euclid. The algebra is better.

In my class are Agnes and lots of big boys Robert Hector is top of the class and sometimes helps me with my latin. Charles is in a low class and has a lady teacher. He and a long thin boy called Leslie are always bottom and always kept in. Lots board with Mr. Hector in a school house. It used to be the old messing house for the militery of long ago Pop says. Near it is the jail. Vi always feels sorry for the thin dogs in the street and brings all the crusts in her pocket too feed them

There is also a young man called Eddy keeping a butcher shop. We see him when we go to school. He talks to us. There are two dear old ladies called Miss henshnam and an old father called a Cannon. They live in a teeny weeny house with the loveliest things in it. They are very nice to us. The Bank mans name is Browner. Near the Convent is another hotel called masonic. Wallace keeps it.

He has lots of boys. The lunaticks are divided into 2 kinds. The tame and the savige. The tame ones men walk in the streets and pull little carts. A warder goes with them. They look like convicts becos of there clothes. In the afternoon the warders take the loons for walks. Men walk on the flats outside the town, ladies walk on the Alice side. It must be a great worry to take so many loonaticks for a walk every day.

Near the residensy is the fort and the house where Doc Conry lives. He is the head of loonaticks. He is very nice Mrs. Conry too. I take her violets we have millons of violets in our garden. But it is not a plesure to take them to her becos always loons are working in her garden without a warder. Even Charles is afraid. He says they can go wild in a second and hit you on the head with the spade. In Dr. C. garden is the fort. Long ago F.B. was a very great place for fighting but only with kafers. Miss Henshman remebers when she rode on a horse and saw the chief Kreli. She was a girl with long golden hair. He talked with her and said I like your long golden hair She remebers when all the soldiers lived here and had red coats not kaki and the band played in the grove. If only they still lived here and played. But all that gets played in the grove now is lots of tennis and crokey.

The shape of the Residensy is like a square. Only at the back-side of the house is a high wall with a high gate in it. The kitchen is one end and far away on othere end the bedrooms. In the middle are the many rooms like big courthouses. They are dining room and sitting room and not much furnitcher becos of being so poor and Pop having so many chuldren. At night the big rooms are frighting to us for they are no windows at the back only loop hole places where they use to shoot out of at the kafers. Richard the constabel who sits in Pops office tells us stories of the wars. He says long ago when the fighting was heavy many dead redcoats lay in the big rooms also wounded. In the big stone bath room where it is so cold was the place for lying out before they buried. That is indeed a nasty place. We dont care much to bath there. Always I think of the poor dead soldiers.

We have a tenis court and lots of trees. We sit in the tree which hangs over the front gate of the drive. We watch when Mr. Rector comes to visit on his bicycle, then we all run even Cootie as hard as we can to the stabels. Vilet runs too. Her mother is dead. She lives with aunt and father. Her father is Vickery the lawyer. Violet and I have made a newspaper. Pop gave us lots of foolscap and nibs and ink. Violet will write the stories and I will write the news. Violet will draw too. We sell it at sixpence each. It is hard work doing so much writing. Charles is useless to write. We write on Friday night when Pop and Mom go to parties. Violet sleeps with us.

Charles has made birdlime again with gum he gets out of the cactus trees on the comonage. We go to the stabel with Piet the groom to boil the gum in tins on the fire. It looks like thick milk. It is messy to put on sticks. Charles nagged at Pop till he bought him a trap cage. He puts a singin bird in and takes it to the veld to call other birds. They come and sit on the bird lime sticks and get caught. Then we put them in a big cage in the garden where they all sing. They are cape canareys, blackheads and geel sysies. Now he has 20 blackheads.

A dredful thing came to us this week all becos of Richard telling us ghosts storeys and one that lives in this house since it was a horspital. It is a poor redcoat whose feet were shot off my mistake and he walks round the gravel walk by the big tank making a strange moaning. Richard made the noise. We all got the cold shivers. When it is light we never think of ghosts but at night when the candles blow in the big rooms and everything is so dark and there are strange noises, Mr. Nailhards furnitcher makes cracking loud noises like guns shooting, then we all think of ghost.

On Friday we were writing the newspaper in the dining room table, when the furnitcher made a great louder crack and 'then all was very quiet then we heard the ghost walking on the gravel outside and making the strange noise Richard made and Florence said I hear the ghost. And Charles said dont be silly there is no ghost and then we heard it again and the wind making a funny noise in the loop holes. Cootie was asleep in the faraway bedroom and we said softly if the ghosts went there what would she do. Then we all got up together and ran to the bedroom and we were all afraid not knowing what to do. Then Violet said. Leave Cootie sleeping on the bed and Charles and Florence will get underneath the other bed and you and I will go under Cootie's bed to look after her. If the ghost comes it will not see any of us Charles put the matches in his pocket and blew out the candle. We all staid still for a long time. Then Charles said what is Florence chewing. She said only the paper I found in the hole in the wall it has a bitter taste. Charles said that is the paper with the rough on rats poison Pop put to kill rats and Violet said she will die in agony what will we do and I said give her lots of milk to drink like when we gave our cat to throw up the poison. And I forgot of the ghost and ran away to the kitchen to get milk. She drank the whole jug and could not throw up. Vi said we must act we must go at once to fetch a doctor. She will die. And Florence cried loudly I do not want to die. Cootie woke up and cried loudly too. Charles rolled her in the tablecloth and put her on his back. Vi and I held Florence by the hand and we came to the front door. When we opened it was very dark and then we heard the ghost walking again and Vi said I am afraid to go up that long drive But Florence cried I dont want to die. So we held hands and shut our eyes and ran hard. Charles had it hard with Coot on his back. Then we came to Bank House where the party was and Mr. Browner opened the door and said who are these dredful children like tramps and Florence howled I have eaten the rough on rats and Pop came out and said God they are mine. Then· we went inside and every one came round and we told about the ghost. They said poor children and Pop said I never put poison anywhere I am not such a fool with children like you. So we sat under the stairs and ate cake. Mom said we disgraced her. We all got rowings when we were going home. We went to bed and Pop went to stabel to see if Naughty was alright and Mom got a jug and went to tap water at tank and all of a sudden she let out a loud screech and came running calling Cecil Cecil there is a ghost and we all jumped up and ran too and Pop took the lantern to look for it and found the ghost. It was only a great piece of tar paper the men had left behind the tank and when the wind was blowing it over and over on the gravel it made a noise like a ghost walking. Pop gave us each a penny and said we had earned it for once. Now we never stay alone. Richard always stays with us but he must not talk of ghosts any more or dead people.

Lots of ladies and men play croket and tenis at the Grove. On Saturdays is the tea day. we go and sit in a little hut on a small hill behind the tea house to watch the playing. Pop says to Mom how are the bacheldor steaks going which old maid will get the prize I said what steaks. There was no meat there today and what is the prize. But no one told me. We have lots of visiters here Mrs. Simms and Vida and Zita. We all went to a fancy ball in the town hall up the stairs. We didnt get any prizes only a girl Pixie being dressed like a turk lady and a girl dressed like a kafer. Miss Pedlar and Miss Molly Holiday danced with us. They are going to have a dancing class in our big room so that all children can learn to do the wals and the paddie car and the lancers. We were not pleased but Mom said one day you will be greatful to me. Charles says who will be greatful to learn to hold girls round the middle and turn like a top. We have to bath and wash and dress up to go to this class.

Mrs. Haman and Mr. H. Came to stay with us. He is the magistrat at Adelaide. He said he would show Pop how to graft rose trees. He took a sharp knife. We all wanted to see how he graffs rose trees but Pop said Get away all of you. So we climbed quickly in the tree to see better and Florence leaned over too much when Mr H was grafing and fell down on top of him and broke her arm and Mr. H cut his thumb. We never saw the end of the graffing.

A merry go round has come. This is the first time we see it. We all wanted to ride on the horses and ducks. but Mom says you will get diseases and it costs money for rides. So Charles went on the top of the m.g.r. with other big boys and kafers to turnturn the big wheel to make it go round and then he could have rides for nothing. But when he had finished turning he ran and lay on the grass and looked a funny colour in his face. He said it was not worth a ride to feel like that.

A great Trajedy has come to the birds. In the night something dug a hole in our avery and killed 13 capies and 16 blackheads. Charles was mad with rage. We buried them in our pets grave-yard and he wrote on the plank Here lies my 16 blackits who all met their death in one nite and Pop looked and said this spell-ing is a disgrace after all the money I pay for you. On Sunday afternoon when everyone sleeps we found a big pot of Mr. Nail-hards black paint in the store. We painted our names on the stone wall of the back stoep. It measured nearly 2 yards for each name. Charles said lets make it big. We used up all the paint then we went to play. Only the next day Pop saw the painting.

It is the worst thing we have ever done. Nothing can take off the names now. Mom said it will go down for time of these awful Vaughan children, why must I have such devils. Our punishment is a hard one. Now must we go to Sunday School every Sunday.

We have been to a horse races on the Flats. Mom and Pop went in the spider. Charles rode on his bicycle. Florence and I went with Mrs. conry in a cart with 2 big horses belonging to a big man with beard called Eddie Niland. He drove us himself. He is a farmer at Kromme and has the best racing horses. Everyone came to the races. There was a big tent where ladies sat to see the horses winning. Pop was a judge sitting in a little kind of box with another man. Long ago befor I was born Pop had racing horses but it wasted too much money so he had to stop. Mom says that is why we are poor now. We sat at the carts with all the other children. A funny man called John came to see his children and made jokes with us. A great shouting came when Eddies horse Kritzinger won. He was called after a Boer general. He is a beautiful chesnut shining like gold. When he won Eddie opened bottles and shampane was drunk. Mom gave out the prizes. Eddie has 2 boys, one is that long boy Leslie who is always being kept in with Charles. He is like Roland thinking a lot of himself but he ought to rember about always being kept in when he thinks a lot of himself. Charles dont think a lot of himself. Last night Charles found out that it is a dog that comes to our avery. Richard said a good plan was to catch the dog and tie a tin to its tail it would never come back again and the birds would be safe. We waited in the trees all the afternoon and saw him come again. We caught him and Charles tied a sardin tin to his tail while I sat on his head. He ran up the road hard and round a corner. It was a great mistake. We are going to have great troubel. Pop and Mom were calling at Mr. Wats house when the dog with the tin came. It was Mr. W dog. He is Mr. W. of this street. He said This is a wicked deed the Police must trace the culprits and Pop came and he talked a lot about this wicked deed all wicked deed all the supper time. We are all afraid what will happen when the Police find that we did this wicked deed. Richard came last night. He said not to worry. He was the policeman looking for the culpret and will never betray us. Now we are safe.

RETURN TO ADELAIDE

We are going back to Adelaide. another shift on. becos Mr. Nailhard and Merry have come back to F.B. I am glad to have an end to Mr. Rector and Sunday School. Only one thing was nice in his Sunday school, it was the librery. Here I got lots to read of all kinds of books 3 a week. When we came back to Adelaide lots of things were different. Mr. Damp has gone away for ever and a new parson has come. His name is Osman cookson and he has a daughter Trissie who is to marry with an inspector of the Police in Utenhage called Bawtree. Pop is building our new house on erfs near the school. A house is also building for Mr. Cookson by the Church so that he can bring his wife and all his people from England to live here. Mr. Cook is not like Mr. Damp He is an old man with a little short beard and eyes which are laughing at you. He knows about children having 5, also, and not good ones. But they are all old. He does not wish to push us in the choir. Pop said do you sing and he said I do not sing I dont know the difference between God save the King and Pop goes the weesel. This was the nicest thing we ever heard a parson say. Mr. Bob thinks he will also build a house on his erfs and a new hotel will be built near the market bell and the train is coming to Adelaide quite soon. Already they are making the bridge for it over near the Old Mill. Every Sunday we all walk to look at it with the pointer dogs. The man who is making it is called Mr. Ropkiss. But he is a coward. When he went with Pop to walk on the piece of bridge which is hanging over the river he got giddy and sat down and a trolly had to come out and fetch him. Men who make bridges ought not to feel like that charles says. Mr. Ropkiss has a daughter with lots of long gold hair called Muriel. They don't stay here all the time. Mr. Ropkiss is busy.

Last Sunday Florence and Coot nearly died on the bridge. They sat on a trolly and Charles said I will push you a little way for a nice ride but when the trolly started it would not stop and Florence screeched and Pop saw and ran with his coat tails flying and pushed his Irish blackthorn walking stick he likes so much under the front for the trolly to stop. Just in time or it would have gone over the bridge far into the river below and Florence and Coot would have their necks broken. All that was broken was the blackthorn it was cracked. But Pop was savige with Charles for doing such a thing Charles never told that he nearly broke his neck when he and Alec and Norman and others went riding on Saturday with Mr. Ropkiss on a trolly and a engine came round Kowie river and nearly ran into them and Mr. Rop screamed Jump and they all jumped and rolled down a great high bank and the trolly was run over by the engine. Charles could not walk nicely for a whole week becos of his knee.

Dr. Jock has many beehives some like little houses. Pop also likes to keep bees. But he is afraid of bees and always has some one to put the swarms in the boxes. Dr. Jock puts a net over his head and gloves on his hands and makes a big smoke when he works with his bees to make them drunk. When our new house is finished we will have hives like Dr. J. with little slides so we can pull them and see through the glass how bees make honey.

Many Weary Willies come now to our house when sun sets to ask for help. Pop says Iris write to Mr. Jailer that he gives a night lodging and pauper ration for this man in the jail. A Weary willies right name is tramp. Pop signs the paper and the weary willies go to sleep in the jail. Also we have many poor people come to our house to complain about their wives who fight them. The one who comes to our house to complain most is Mr. we call him Hakkelaar becos he stuttering. Sometimes Pop gives him a long lectur and sometimes he gives his wife a good rowing and talks about Paul in the Bible who says wives obey your husbands Pop says they are a dam nuisance to him. The other day they both came together. We ran and said here come all two hakkelaars to see you. They both talked at once and Mr. H said Mr. Vaughan she jes took a mok and kepped me on my koup. Look how she scryched me. And we laughed so loud Pop chased us away and we not hearing any more. Hakkelaar told us all about catching swarms of bees. He knows. Next time we have a swarm he will

He knew about bees.

put it in the little hive with the glass window becos Pop helps him with his wife.

We saw a clever thing the big men did for celebrating. They made large balls with string and put them in tar and parafeen and lit them and threw them about the square. They made a lovely light and roaring noise. Pop says they dam dangerous things.

This week the most wonderful thing is to happen to Adelaide. The railway is opening at last. Everyone who wants is going in a train without paying to have a picnic at Apies Draai near Bedford. Mrs. Davidson and Mrs. Will and us are packing our baskets together. Everyone is making parties to be together at the picnic. The train came and stood in the station. All got in their own carriag. Rena Sparks was most brave. She sat in a window and never fell out but the train went slowly all the way. Charles showed us where the engine ran over the troly. When we got to Apies Draai we all got out and had a lovely picnic place. In the afternoon Pop and Dr. Jock came in the spider and lots of people from Bedford. Then the train came back and we all went home singing all the way. Now we go sometimes at night to see the train when it comes in. Lots go to see. It has not yet started to go to F.B.

A terribel thing happened about Hakkelaar and the bees. He came to take the swarm that sat in the tree near our water tank and put it in hive. There were visitors talking in the parlor so we helped him. He must first catch the queen. But he never tied his sleeves or put a net or made a smoke like Dr. Charles said you must tie your trousers on the legs but he would not listen. Then we all stood near the house becos we know what Doc said about swarming bees being dangeros. And then when Hakelar was shaking the swarm the queen bee flew out and went up his trouser and all the bees swarmed round him and he began to ran and lossened his belt and we all ran in the bathroom and looked out of the window and he pulled off his shirt and screamed and Charles shouted pull off your trousers you fool and he pulled off everything and jumped in the water barrel by the tank and just then Pop and Mom came round the corner and the visitors to look at the grape vine and we shouted go away He has no clothes on and is in

Hakkelaar all the bees swarmed round him.

58

the barrel becos the bees are dangeros and Pop ran in the house and all the others too. The bees all swarmed on top of the trousers and Andries came and made a smoke and got the quuen out and put the swarm in and then Hakkelaar could have his clothes back again. Doctor says he is lucky not being stung to death. Mom says this is most scandelous thing that has happened and may it be a lesson to Pop and his having the bees.

A new teacher has come to the school. He is a very nice man with lots of children. He is called McGaffin He has Ken and Bobbie and Dodo and Trevor and Charlie. He is letting us have a tennis and hockey court at school. Miss Maggie and Miss Hilda Sparks help us with the tennis and when we go in a donkey wagon to play at Bedford. We start in the morning when it is still dark and nearly alwys win. Charles has gone for a holiday to Macazana. His friends are Willie and Drissi Meyer. There are many Meyers. I have not yet got them right. There are also many Pearsons and Morgans. I cannot get them right either. Charles says in this Macazana live the nicest of all people and the best farms. No one rows you there. You ride horses all day and go to tennis party and a church at Glenthorn.

Others live in this valley Bennetes and Leppans and Harebottles. One farmer loves this valley so much he is always driving around in it. Charles says someone sent him a letter with Mr. Farmer up and down the Macazana written on it and it found him and he was in a rage. I wouldn't be. The farms have strange names like Jerico Whitebank Black Hill Linton and somewhere a Spring Valley. Charles says some very nice men come to visit there Chappy Scott Ted Frames Jack Porter. They play nice music and sing nice songs. One of the songs they sing is There is a garden fair over the eastern sea and Oh my dolores youll be waiting for me by the eastern sea in the shade of a pine tree. They also sing a fine song about Comrades comrades ever since we were boys sharing our sorrow and joys. Pop says we get on his nerves singing this flora dora songs. We wish we could hear them singing. They make the music for the dancing after the tennis party and cricket. We have never stayed on a farm. It must be wonderful to see milk coming out of lots of cows and scratching the cream off it when it is cold and having so many horses to ride and no one to row you all day.

A new man has come to work in Pops office. He is Mr. Douglas. He comes from Seymour. He likes poetry like Pop likes poetry. Some night he sits by our fire and reads to us out of Shakespear. Also a chemist has come to have a shop near Midgleys Hotel. He is a very short man and has many children. his name is Godfrey.

We had a party last night in our dining room. Capt. Glinn came from Alice. Every month Inspector of Police comes. He was at the party. He is a very big man with a big pointed mustash sticking out like wires at each end. I am glad Pops mustach does not stick out in wires. He still had his spurs on at the party

59

Inspector of Police.

as he did not have time to change being so late. He danced a strange kind of new dance with Miss Cookson called a Cakewalk on the stoep Bending backwards and clapping hands and bending forward and holding hands. It Was so strange we all looked round the corner. It is a thing coons dance in America. Why cake walk. Florence and Coot went to bed after that. Charles and I had to do our homework. Lots of singing went on. A man sang a night has a 1000 eyes and Mrs. Gee sang a loud loud song about Angus Macdonald is coiming home from a war and all of a sudden I heard a strange roaring noise in the passage and I saw a great light and it was Florence and Coot in their pajamas throwing fireballs we had made at each other and one fireball stuck in the curten which is in front of the dining room door and it set alight and I ran and pulled at it and Florence and Coot screeched and jumped under the blankets and pretending to go to sleep and Charles ran and kicked the fireballs out of the front door in the garden and jumped on them and Pop came and said My God and the party people screamed Fire. Then it was all over and only the burnt curten and my fingers with blister and for once Charles and I didnt get a rowing for making the troubel at all.

Now we are having a very nice new kind of thing of school. It is called drilling. Pops new Sarge his name is Jackson came to Mr. McGaff and told him all about this drilling and Mr. McGaff said all children go home and tell your parents and bring a note tomorrow if you must do this drilling. Pop said yes we must it is good for mussels musles musels. We all have to wear blue pleeted skirts and blouses and white tackies on the feet and drill with wood dumb bells and broom sticks. Sarge says Fall in and we all fall in then he says Shun and we all stand up strait. At the end we march and then he says doubel and we have to run fast and faster making shapes like snakes and 8s and rows and rings. It is the nicest kind of school I have ever had. All the boys laughed

60

A long song about Angus Macdonald.

and called us Jacksons girls. Now they must drill too so they dont laugh any more.

A new butcher shop has started here. Eddie Webb who was in Fort Beaufort when we were there and Chicken Edwards whose mother lives at the drift have started it. Charles is friends of both and help them when school is over. Here they do a dredful thing to poor ducks. They nail ducks on planks through the webs in their toes and all day someone must go and feed ducks with thick porrige pushing it down the throats. This is to make them nice and fat for Xmas. Chiken says if ducks run about and do much quaking they will never have fat on for Xmas and no one will buy thin ducks. So ducks must be nailed fast and stuff. I am glad we eating turkey for Xmas and not poor fat ducks Pop has 2 hen turkeys not for eating, for sitting on eggs to hatch fowls chickens. Pops does this to turkeys. He gives them a good strong drink of brandy, pouring it down the beak. The turkey shuts its eyes and makes much gaping then Pop puts it in dark box in wagon house to sit on 24 eggs. Then the turkey feels so nice with the brandy in it that it is silly and thinks it is broody and sits nicely on many eggs which is better than one hen sitting on only 12 eggs Pop says.

A great thing happened here this week. The governor Sir Hely

Huchinson came to open out new Town Hall on the Square. It was wonderful A band came to play and carts were decorated to fetch Gov from station and much nice food was eaten and speechifying was given by Mr. Mayor and Pop and other men from parlement All school children came and stood in rows to listen but not to eat. Then we all ran to station to see Gov get on the train again He was a short man with a red face and a nice mustach like Pops Every one must call him by a strange name Your Excelencly. Why Excelencely. When we saw him standing and talking to Pop and Mom on platform by the train Charles and I ran to him and said Mr. Excelencely will you please ask Mr. Mcgaff to give us a holiday today becos of the opening of the new Town hall. And Mr. Ex laughed and said what is your name and Pop said these dredful children belong to me, and Mr. Ex said to Mr. Mcgaff who was there too I think they could all have a holiday today becos I know what it is to be young. And so we had a holiday and all were pleased but Mom said we always disgracing her becos Charles face was begrimed with the dirt and my hair was hanging wild all over my face and my pinafor was dirty. Always my hair is a worry becos of the ribbin falling off and getting lost. When I ran to the station it fell off.

Many new people are coming to Adelaide and another hotel is being built where Mr. Sam Brown made the cofins. It will be called the Central hotel. Mr. seliger is coming to look after it. He has many children too. Hetty and Gertie and Minnie and Erna and two boys. Pop is giving a cricket cup for playing for between Adelaide and Bedford. Much fighting goes on when Adelaide and Bedford are playing the football match, but not when they playing cricket. Our cricket is the best, but some of the farmers in Kromme are good too they learning at school in Gramstown.

In this October I will be 13 years old. Mr. McGaff says I am to write the Elementary Exam this year. I must work hard and no more nonsense This Euclid is the thing I must work the hardest There will not be much time to write any more. Today Florence was teaching Coot to do the Cake walk and let her fall on her head. They were both punished. Florence is a very rough kind of child always making much troubel. She let Coot fall out of the swing on her back and Coot was lying so still she came to Mom and said you better come and look at Coot she is now dead. But Coot was not quite dead. She was only stunned and had to go to bed for some days. Pop was so savige he cut the swing down. Charles and I got the free tickets for a play in the town hall. I have never seen a play with men and women acting in it. It was wonderful. It was called the BELLS When it was over I could not speak it was so wonderful. All the way home I was thinking of that poor man who stole the money becos his people were poor and the terribel words he said when he was so unhappy. He said Oh God put back the universe and give me yesterday. I hope I may never feel like that man and say those terribel words.